THE HAMLYN
POCKET DICTIONARY OF WINES

THE HAMLYN

POCKET DICTIONARY OF

———————— ★ ————————

WINES

John Paterson

HAMLYN

LONDON · NEW YORK · SYDNEY · TORONTO

First published in 1980 by
The Hamlyn Publishing Group Limited
London · New York · Sydney · Toronto
Astronaut House, Feltham, Middlesex, England

ISBN 0 600 39498 0

Phototypeset by Tradespools Limited, Frome, Somerset.
Printed in Great Britain by
Hazell Watson & Viney Ltd, Aylesbury, Bucks.

Distributed in the U.S. by
Larousse & Co. Inc., 572 Fifth Avenue, New York,
New York 10036.

Contents

Introduction

How Wine is Made

In spite of the mystique that has come to surround it, wine is a fairly simple beverage to make. It can be summed up in three words: fermented grape juice. And this, indeed, is how wine is legally defined in many countries.

Fermentation is a process in which sugar is converted into alcohol and carbon dioxide. Each grape skin has tens of thousands of wine yeast cells and several million wild yeast cells, as well as moulds and bacteria. When the grapes are crushed the yeasts attack the natural sugar in the grape juice, and the transformation of the sugar into alcohol and carbon dioxide begins. Ultimately, the yeasts are killed off and what remains is a solution of water, alcohol and various other constituents, including traces of minerals, phosphates, acids and tannin.

Red wine is made from black grapes. Their juice, like that of white grapes, is colourless. The colour comes from the pigment in the grape skins, which are allowed to remain in the fermenting juice.

Rosé wine is also made from black grapes. In this case the skins are allowed to remain in contact with the juice for only a short period, after which the fermenting juice is transferred to another vat. Sometimes rosé is made by blending red and white wines.

White wine may be made from white or black grapes, but the skins are immediately separated from the juice.

All these wines, red, white and rosé, are then left to mature in cask before going into bottle. The period of cask maturation is variable. Some wines are bottled after six months, while others may spend three or four years in cask. Many wines then need several years in bottle to attain further maturity.

White, red, or rosé wines can be made to sparkle, but white sparklers are by far the most popular. The best are made by the method used by the producers of Champagne – the *méthode champenoise*. Still wine is bottled with a dose of yeast and sugar solution to promote a second fermentation in bottle. The bubbles of carbon dioxide created by this second fermentation are imprisoned in the bottle, to emerge in a golden, foaming tumult when the bottle is ultimately opened by the customer.

This method is a costly one because it is labour-intensive. Over a prolonged period the sediment is shaken down the bottle until it reaches the base of a temporary cork. When this has been achieved the neck of the bottle is frozen and the cork removed, along with the frozen sediment. Then the wine is given a dose of sweetening and the permanent cork inserted.

Two other important methods are used to make sparkling wine. In the *cuve close*, or 'closed tank', method the secondary fermentation takes place in a large tank and the wine is then filtered and bottled under pressure. In the *transvasement*, or transfer system, the wine undergoes its second fermentation in bottle, but is then transferred to a pressure tank for filtering.

Some wines, red, white or rosé, have a slight sparkle. This is sometimes a natural development in the wine, but it is more likely to have been deliberately induced by the use of particular methods of vinification.

Fortified wine is made by the addition of brandy either during or after the fermentation period. In the case of port, the object is to end the fermentation so that a proportion of natural sugar from the grapes remains. The addition of brandy to sherry helps to preserve the wine and adjust its character.

The Vintage

Weather is all important to the wine grower, as it is to any other farmer. There are wine lands where the weather is dependable year after year, so that the quality and character of the wine changes hardly at all. A vintage date on the label is mainly valuable as a pointer as to whether the wine is mature. A grower in such assured climates will have security, but he will never make the greatest wines.

In Germany and much of France it is different. Here the makers of the world's most prized wines perpetually walk a tightrope between a great vintage and one that is below standard. Freak weather can make or break a vintage.

This is why fine wines are remembered in terms of years as well as names. One year's wine is never the same in all respects as that of another. The weather works its alchemy on the grapes; next year it will work it another way.

In some years the weather will make an abundant crop, in others it will produce a lean one. But quantity is not decisive in wine-making; a plentiful harvest can make poor wine just as a meagre harvest can make great wine.

All kinds of extremes in the weather can affect the vintage. Frost in the spring can cripple the vines, hail in the summer can decimate the grapes and too much cloud and rain can leave them unripe. Grapes need sunlight to develop their sugar content and warmth to bring down their acid level. When they get too much or too little, they will be unbalanced. Weather conditions also have an important effect on the length of time wine needs to reach maturity.

As well as great and poor vintages, there are good vintages and average ones. There are also mixed vintages, in which the different areas of a region like Bordeaux, for example, can produce wines showing considerable variations in quality.

All this would seem to call into question the validity of vintage charts of the kind shown on page 254, because in every vintage there are exceptions to the general rule. Charts do, however, give a broad picture of the general quality of the wine made in the different regions year by year and for that reason they are a useful guide, particularly for those planning to buy wine for laying down to reach maturity.

In Champagne, and in the port region of Portugal, vintages are 'declared' by the individual producer only when he considers the wine of any one year to be of exceptional merit. Most Champagnes and ports are blended from the wine of several years, and carry no vintage date.

Authenticity and Quality

One way or another most wine-producing countries have a system aimed at preventing the counterfeiting of wines, a practice once so widespread that it became a serious threat to the reputation of the legitimate producer.

Many countries have based their wine controls on the French *Appellation d'Origine Contrôlée* (AC or AOC) system. This is a series of rules which stipulate, among other things, the districts, parishes and in some instances even individual plots which are entitled to prestigious wine placenames.

As well as being concerned with authenticity, the wine laws in most countries set down certain minimum standards which have an impact on the quality of wine. It is not possible, for example, for a Burgundy producer to decide that the grape variety he grows is too troublesome to cultivate and too unproductive, uproot it and plant something easier to tend and more productive, yet still use the Burgundy appellation. The French laws specify the variety of grapes permitted in each AC area. They also control viticultural methods like pruning and fertilizing. They lay down the minimum alcoholic strength of wines and the maximum yield in hectolitres per hectare in order to overcome the temptation to overproduce at the cost of quality. The laws also specify methods of vinification, most usually those that are traditional in the district, though modern methods may obtain approval.

It is not possible, of course, to legislate for wine to be of consistently high quality, since there are differences in the standard of wine produced in each year's vintage. But in general the French system, and other systems modelled on it, do provide a degree of assurance to the consumer that it will have met certain minimum standards.

Italy's DOC (*Denominazione di Origine Controllata*) system is much the same as the French one. It came into operation only in 1963, but since then has done much to increase the confidence of overseas buyers in the quality and authenticity of Italian wines. Sales to the UK have increased dramatically.

Germany's wine laws are of particular assistance to the consumer, being as much concerned with quality as with authenticity. A quality league of wines runs from *Tafelwein*, plain table wine, at the lowest end, up to *Qualitätswein mit Prädikat*, quality with a special distinction, at the top.

Thus the reputation of a vineyard is not the principal criterion when it comes to selecting German wine, for the vineyard that produces

Qualitätswein in one vintage could, if its wine is substandard at the next vintage as a result of unfavourable weather conditions, have all its wine from that vintage demoted by the authorities to *Tafelwein*.

The Law and the Label

Regulations laid down by the European Economic Community are designed to protect the consumer by requiring specific information to be shown on wine bottle labels. The regulations also permit a good many optional extras, which the producer, shipper or bottler can print on the label if he so wishes. What is not on the list of permitted extras has to be regarded as prohibited.

The compulsory information on still, light wines bottled and sold in the EEC is, firstly, a statement of contents in metric terms; secondly, the country of origin; thirdly, the name and address of the bottler; and fourthly, a concise product description. This last need be no more, in the case of ordinary wines, than 'table wine' or its equivalent in French, German or Italian. Quality wines must carry the name of their specified region of origin and one of the approved terms of quality – for example, *Vin délimité de qualité supérieure* or *Appellation contrôlée*, in the case of

French wines; *Qualitätswein* or *Qualitätswein mit Prädikat*, for German products, and *Denominazione di origine controllata* or *Denominazione di origine controllata e garantita* for Italian wines.

All these terms, and there are several others, are, of course, a guarantee of the authenticity of the contents of the bottle, and no one is likely to omit them from his labels if he is entitled to use them.

In Britain the regulations are monitored by the Wine Standards Board. The Board was set up by the ancient Vintners' Company of the City of London, which historically had wide supervisory and disciplinary powers in the wine trade. The opportunity to revive this role came when the EEC required member states to enforce the wine laws and ensure their proper implementation. The Board, with a team of inspectors throughout the country keeping an eye on bottlers and shippers, acts as agent for the Ministry of Agriculture. It is the Ministry, on the advice of the Board, which decides whether prosecutions should be made. Many of the dubious practices that have been uncovered are dealt with by firm persuasion and prosecutions have been fairly rare.

There are still some EEC wines available which do not conform to all the EEC's descriptive requirements. These are, for the most part, pre-1977 vintage reds, which were bottled and labelled before the implementation of the law.

The optional extras that can be used in light wine descriptions include a statement of alcoholic strength, an indication of whether the wine is red, white, rosé, sweet or dry, and the use of a brand name. These, however, must not be likely to give a misleading impression. A shipper will not be allowed to use a contrived name that could be confused with one of the recognized areas of production.

The mandatory information that must be given with non-EEC wines is similar to that required of EEC wines.

Bottle Contents

Bottle contents have always differed between one country and another, and even between different regions of the same country. Standardization of contents is one of the objectives of the European Economic Community and already there have been moves in that direction. The 75-cl bottle is likely to emerge as the standard for light wines. At present, capacity usually ranges from 70 cl to 75 cl. Champagne bottles have to be larger than standard because they are designed to withstand considerable pressure from within. They have a capacity of 80 cl. Magnums and other outsize bottles will also be standardized, probably up to five litres for light wines and three for sparkling wines. EEC regulations now require that wine labels must show the capacity of bottles.

At present, the contents of outsize bottles, expressed in terms of the approximate contents of standard-sized bottles, are:

Litre	$1\frac{1}{2}$
Magnum	2
Double magnum or Jeroboam (Champagne)	4
Jeroboam (Bordeaux)	5
Rehoboam	6
Imperial or Methuselah	8
Salmanazar	12
Balthazar	16
Chantigianna (Italy)	$2\frac{1}{3}$
Toscanello (Italy)	$2\frac{2}{3}$

Wine Tastings

Tastings were once only for the wine trade or for important customers like caterers and club committees. They were rather serious occasions, with conversation largely confined to business topics. These days, however, many tastings are intended expressly for the public. They are much more social affairs than trade tastings, but still serious. Tastings of this kind are a good way of tracking down agreeable bottles.

There are, for example, numerous shippers who sell direct to the public and who are able to offer advantageous prices because their overheads are low. Some catch the attention of the public by advertising and some hold tastings, while others do both these things. Tastings are also often organized by high street retailers, wine clubs and the promotional agencies of wine-producing countries.

Wine tastings are a great deal less complex than they seem. The customer is simply on the lookout for a wine that pleases him and of which he would like to have more.

It is sensible not to attempt to sample too many wines at one tasting and ideally, no more than a dozen or so should be offered. If the number on show significantly exceeds that figure it is important to be selective. After sampling about a dozen wines, the palate has a tendency to become jaded; it cannot assess accurately any more.

It is unlikely that at a public tasting one will need to judge whether a wine is ready for drinking, or has passed its peak, or is simply 'off'. The wines on offer at public tastings are, as a rule, all for current drinking. No merchant who wants to stay in business will be showing declining or disordered wines.

Tips on what to watch for need to be generalized, for differing groups and nationalities of wines all have their individual characteristics, and what may be a good point in one may be less good in another. In dry and medium white wines, beware of those that taste mouth-wateringly sharp. This is usually the result of excessive acidity. Dry whites should have sufficient acid to be piquant, but not so much as to be sour. Less common are whites suffering from too little acidity: the clue to this is a dull, flabby flavour.

Nearly all reds, even though they may be judged by the merchant to be ready for current drinking, can show some improvement in bottle. Thus a little bitterness is not amiss and should disappear in a few months, or even a few weeks. But avoid reds that taste rough or shallow or that have a watery finish. These are flaws that will never be ironed out.

The tasting formula is straightforward enough. First swirl the wine in the glass to release the bouquet. Then sniff it – good wines, whether red, white or rosé, should have an appetizing bouquet. Sip the wine, holding it in the mouth to savour it. Most organizers of tastings provide spittoons or boxes filled with sawdust. Spitting is the prudent course at a tasting featuring young wines that still need to mature, or one at which an extensive variety of wine styles is being shown. But swallowing is in order when a small range of wines of a similar style is presented.

Faults in Wine

There is good wine, indifferent wine and bad wine and every vintage produces its quota of each, in one degree or another. Nothing in wine making has any certainty about it. The shape of wine owes more to nature than it owes to the skill, or lack of skill, of the wine maker.

But accidents do happen with wines as they do with any other kind of product. Sometimes they can be remedied, sometimes not. A bottle that fails to respond to the remedies suggested here should be taken back as quickly as possible to the supplier, who should replace it or refund its cost without question.

The main retail operators in the UK instruct their branch managers to go along with the customer so far as complaints are concerned, but clearly there are limits. There are wines with sediment, most notably among older red wines, which are not faulty. Some wines are intended to have sediment and would, indeed, be suspect should they be without it. There are corks that smell musty, but this is only a normal manifestation in red wines that have spent some time in bottle. There are corks that look so brand new that they might have been inserted at the instant the wine was bought. But a lot of plainer wines are bottled in Britain and may have been in bottle for only a few weeks before they reached the off-licence shelves. There is nothing exceptionable about new, pristine corks or elderly, stained corks. Age or youth are not causes for complaint.

These are some of the objections that retailers and merchants get about their wines. There are plenty of others, but the important thing is that the volume of complaints is quite small. The British wine trade is one of the most experienced, skilful and perceptive in the world, and this includes major wine-producing countries, as well as minor ones. Complaints are few and justifiable complaints even fewer.

The merchant, off-licence manager or other supplier will not, however, be so complacent that he will shrug off a customer's complaint. He will take it seriously. Or at any rate he will take it seriously if the evidence looks convincing. A bottle that is a half or two-thirds empty will hardly be the most convincing piece of evidence to present to him.

These are the main faults that may occasionally be found in wine:

CORKY (OR CORKED) The cork is diseased or rotting, giving off a general stink and imparting an equally disagreeable flavour to the wine. Bottle and cork should be sent back.

OXIDIZATION Caused by air reaching the wine at some stage during the bottling process as a result of a loose cork. White and rosé wines darken in colour, and any kind of wine will have a bad, sour wine smell and flavour. The customer has only himself to blame if this has happened because he has stored the wine badly at home by allowing the bottle to stand upright for a lengthy period, or storing it in warm sunlight or near a heating unit. Otherwise the wine should be returned at once for replacement.

SECONDARY FERMENTATION This can arise from a chemical change in the wine and can cause a bottle to explode, a good reason for storing wines in bins. This will to some extent protect other bottles in the store from the impact of the explosion. Sometimes only the cork is 'blown', but the contents are lost just the same. Possibly the fermentation will not reach this stage, and its development will be apparent only when the bottle is opened. There is likely to be a disagreeable smell which will also be present in the taste. When the customer has stored the wine, there is little to be done but dispose of it. If it has been newly or recently bought, the retailer should be expected to reimburse the cost.

CLOUDINESS Again, chemical changes in the composition of the wine may be responsible, though sometimes the condition can arise because it has been stored in a draughty place. Open the bottle and sniff it; taste it if necessary. Should these tests reveal nothing undesirable, give the opened bottle an hour or so to clear. If that does not happen, return the bottle and cork to the retailer for a refund or a replacement.

CRYSTALS Some white wines can show small, sparkling flakes which may look like broken glass. Give them an opportunity to disappear, which they may well do. The conditions is caused by an excess of tartrates resulting from a spell in the cold. If they fail to disappear, the bottle should be replaced or the cost refunded.

None of these faults should be regarded as an excuse to reject a bottle and claim a refund. They represent only guidelines and it is worth emphasizing that they are all rarely encountered. It bears repeating that sediment in wine is no more than a natural deposit left by the grapes and that different standards apply in different countries. In Britain the regular drinker of modest red wines does not want, or expect, to find heavy sediment in his wine, and to meet his requirements even the plainest of wines are carefully filtered. Abroad, though, it is a different matter; wine may be cheap because it has not had to pay its way through such a refinement. The man who finds in Spain, for instance, a good two inches of 'sludge' at the foot of his litre bottle of red should console himself that this is all part of the goodness and character of the wine.

Starting a Cellar

Few people have house room for an extensive collection of wines to slumber away until they reach maturity or, to use the shorthand term, to 'lay down' wines. This was the old order of things in town houses and country mansions, when the wine merchant delivered a few dozen cases of vintage wines which were then put down in the cellar and faithfully recorded in the cellar book. The butler was responsible for the wines, kept the keys to the cellar, and was expected to know when each batch of wine was ripe and ready for drinking.

Cellars seldom come with modern houses and butlers hardly at all. Nevertheless, there is no reason why the householder of the 1980s should not venture into the interesting and rewarding pastime of salting away a few cases of wine, provided he has the space and the conditions are right.

It is a matter of economics. Even discounting inflation, wine that will benefit by being matured in bottle will always increase in value as the years roll by. There are two main reasons for this: money invested by traders in young wines could be earning interest if it were otherwise employed, so that in a sense the wine paid for with the money has to earn its 'interest'. And large quantities of bottles occupy large areas of commercial cellar space, which has to pay its own way as well as bear a share of such overheads as rent, rates, lighting, and maintenance. So in normal market conditions producers, middlemen, importers and retailers are anxious to get rid of their wine as soon as possible. Each takes his cut and passes the wine on to the next man. Last man in the chain is the consumer.

Before he can take his 'cut' the consumer has to

wait some time until the wine has reached its peak of maturity. At that point he is able to drink wine for which the man next door would have to pay through the nose if he tried to buy it from a wine merchant and which he might in any case find hard to obtain.

All this, of course, applies to fine wines. Cheap wines, with a very few exceptions, do not improve in bottle, and the majority are more likely to deteriorate.

Even among fine wines there are exceptions. Few whites benefit by being kept in bottle for years; they lose their freshness and will taste dull. Sauternes, on the other hand, can develop magnificently in bottle over a period of many years and emerge as rounded wine with a superlatively silken texture.

But it is among fine red wines and Vintage port that the real rewards are to be found. Two or three years after the vintage the UK wine retailer will offer wines at 'opening prices'. These are naturally higher than opening prices in such centres as Bordeaux or Beaune, because the retailer is not in business to sell wines for the same amount as he paid for them, but the opening price will be the cheapest one for the consumer. When it moves, it will move up.

This, then, is the optimum time to buy. Watch

for wine merchants' 'wines for laying down' proposals and consider them seriously. Consider also the price, compared with that of wines rated to be ready for drinking now on the same merchant's list, and consider the vintage. An indication of the best value can be seen from a vintage chart.

People with house room for only a dozen bottles may lay down wine with advantage, but those with the capacity to accommodate a larger number of bottles are obviously likely to benefit more. All wines must lie horizontally. When a bottle stands upright the cork dries out and shrinks since it is no longer in contact with the wine. This lets the air in and the wine is ruined.

The temperature of a storage area must be reasonably constant, kept at around 13° C (55° F) without dramatic fluctuations, so do not earmark the airing cupboard as a suitable storage area. Keep wine away from any strong-smelling household goods like paint, turpentine or creosote. After a time their smell would penetrate the cork and taint the wine. Areas in which vibration is likely to occur are also to be avoided.

Much of this also applies to wines that are nearing maturity, with two or three years to go. Temperature is less important, but it should still not vary too much.

For those who like to speculate, laying down wine is not necessarily a route to riches. Young wine that has been kept until it is mature will certainly be more valuable than when it was bought. For example, in the period 1968–78 a dozen bottles of Château-Latour rose in price from £42 to £150, and it costs a great deal more now. But the owner cannot sell to the public, unless he has a licence. The most likely way to raise a respectable sum is to send the wine to auction, but then the auctioneer will want his commission. Best to drink it.

Where to Buy

There are two traditional, long-established retail sources of wine for the British consumer, and a good many more that are relatively new and which have played an important part in changing the whole face of wine retailing in the UK.

The longest established in the first category are merchants who may have been in business for two or three centuries. Having survived the vicissitudes of commercial life for such periods, they have only partially responded to cut-price competition. Some offer discounts for dozens, among their medium and lower-priced wines, but because they do a good deal of business with individuals and institutions requiring high-quality wines, it is in this end of the market that many such retailers are most interested. They are good for special services such as renting out cellar space for customers who want to lay down wine, and some will still open a bottle at the request of a known client so that it is ready to be served with dinner the same night. They are also very helpful with polite and well-informed advice, and are likely to have a much larger selection of fine wines than any other readily accessible retail outlet.

Well-established off-licence chains – and there is a branch of one or the other in virtually every significant town in the UK – offer a wide selection of wines, from plain varieties up to those that are highly rated. Prices are reasonably relaxed and often keen, especially among brands or marques in which the owners of the chain (very often brewery companies) have some kind of special interest. They may have the sole agency for importation or perhaps they create a branded wine of their own and are able to buy in bulk from the producer, passing on part of the benefit of the resulting economy to the consumer. The chains have a fair selection, but are not generally strong on high quality. At least one chain, however, has a list of good quality and fine wines. They will not necessarily be available on demand, but the branch manager will have instructions to send an order to head office for any wine on the list that is still available. Branch managers may or may not be able to give informed advice, however. The level of knowledge is variable.

Among the fairly recent additions to retail outlets are wine clubs. Some are independent, in the sense that they are not controlled by or affiliated to the big groups in the business of importing wines and selling them to the public, and are therefore not bound by board-room decisions on what they may buy and sell. Others may have a link, not always overtly, with a major importer, and others again may have a direct and declared link.

In general, the clubs offer good wines at discount prices. Those which give tastings only occasionally or not at all may ask the consumer to take the advice of their own pundits, which is not always satisfactory for wine drinkers who want to form their own opinion. Unless they have complete faith in the observations of the club's 'experts', people who know enough about wine to want to make a personal judgement may prefer to avoid clubs which are shy of tastings. Otherwise it is better to go for a club that offers a taste, even at a fee. Most clubs will want an order of not less than a dozen bottles, though usually the dozen can comprise an assortment of different wines.

One important development beginning in the sixties was the emergence on a significant scale of retailers specializing in cut-price bottles. Some have branches in major centres throughout the UK, while others have up to half a dozen branches or so concentrated in one area. They have, in general, had a beneficial effect, chiefly by helping to encourage more traditional retailers to look at their own pricing policies. Many of the cut-price specialists carry a remarkable variety of stock, ranging from outsize bottles of plain Italian wines up to classified clarets and vintage ports.

There are certainly bargains to be found at such outlets, though it is advisable to compare the prices asked for better-quality wines with those asked by conventional retailers. And wines from 'off' vintages have a way of turning up in some of these shops. Consult a vintage chart, rather than the salesman: advice is not always a strong point in this section of the retail trade.

Advice is not the top attraction of the wine sections of supermarkets, either. These, like the cut-price outlets, are comparative newcomers to wine retailing but they have made a considerable impact on the market with their pricing policies and their practical approach to wine purchasing. Whatever shortcomings they may have over advice, supermarkets sometimes compensate by providing good, written descriptions of the character and style of the wines they offer, either on a back label or neck tag of the bottle, or on shelf notices. At least two of the major supermarket groups are particularly good at this. Others try, and some make no effort at all to advise in any way, tending to stick to mundane, widely advertised brands which they assume will be known to the public.

Supermarket prices are not always particularly favourable and their prices for branded wines, vermouths and proprietary aperitifs should be compared with those of other retailers. A few, however, offer their 'own label' bottles, which may range from party wines in double litres up to Champagne, while in between these two extremities it is possible to find a selection of good French, German, Italian and other wines at reasonable prices. Overall, such wines are carefully chosen and represent good value for money. Supermarkets do not, as a rule, stock fine clarets, Burgundies or Vintage ports.

Mail-order wine dealers are another fairly recent development. Like wine clubs, they are likely to sell in dozens, though again the dozen may not necessarily have to be a 'straight' dozen, but may be an assortment. Many of the merchants selling either exclusively or principally by mail order have a high reputation. Some specialize in the wines that are likely to be difficult to find elsewhere. Prices are usually reasonable.

The mail-order merchants make contact with the public mainly through the columns of newspapers or periodicals and the publishers' organizations vet the status of potential advertisers before advising their members to accept orders for space. The publishers cannot, and do not, assess the quality of the wines offered in the advertisements. So, while a customer has a fair certainty of receiving the goods he orders, there is no guarantee about the quality of them and it is wise to take some precautions.

First, send for the mail-order merchant's list. If it seems to be knowledgeable and informative, and gives some satisfactory indication of the merchant's background, that is a plus. When ordering, do not choose a dozen of one kind of wine, unless you know it is exactly what you want or it has been independently recommended. An assortment of wines should include at least two or three that are pleasing. Finally, it is advisable to respond only to advertisements that appear in established or otherwise reputable newspapers or magazines which will have taken some trouble to ensure the acceptability of the advertiser and his advertisement. This does not rule out advertisements in newly launched publications, but it is as well in these circumstances to check with the publisher on what he knows of the advertiser and his reputation.

It is always worth bearing in mind that some retailers will give discounts for quantity. Wine clubs and mail-order dealers will set these out in their lists. The traditional wine merchants and the off-licence chains may or may not include them in theirs, and some of the chains no longer issue regularly published lists, but it is always worth enquiring. Cut-price merchants and supermarkets are not likely to make any such concessions.

Serving Wine

There are no hard-and-fast rules about serving wine. It is open to anyone to slosh chilly Château-Latour into tumblers and toss it back, sediment and all. But this is not the way to get the maximum enjoyment from fine wine or, come to that, from any wine. As in everything else, there are good ways and bad ways of doing things. The generally accepted procedures for handling and serving wine are based not on meaningless ritualism but on commonsense considerations of how to get the best from it.

Many wines are ready for more or less instant drinking, with no more taxing preparation requirements than that the cork should be drawn. Even in the case of humble wines, though, it is not a bad idea to draw the cork an hour or so before the wine is to be consumed. This gives it a chance to aerate a little, to expand and blossom.

Red wines straight from a draughty off-licence shelf should be given a chance to reach room temperature. This is not likely to be necessary in warm weather when the wine may already be above the temperature of the room, but there is nothing as cheerless in cold weather as a red wine that is cold.

In the case of inexpensive reds, the waiting period can be shortened by placing the opened bottle near a central-heating radiator or by the cooker. Plunging the bottle into hot water has nothing to commend it and none of these short-cut methods is right for better quality reds. They can totally ruin the wine.

White wines need to be cooled, whatever the weather outside. A bottle of dry or medium-dry white wine can spend about 40 minutes in a moderately cold refrigerator. Champagne and other sparklers need a spell of about one hour. Very sweet, still wines, like Sauternes, can take about 35 minutes more. Dry or dryish fortified wines, such as Fino and Amontillado sherry, patent aperitifs, and vermouth, will be freshened by a 40-minute spell in the refrigerator. White port can benefit by the same treatment but Ruby ports are best kept away from the 'fridge. Some older Tawny ports, if they are to be taken as aperitifs, rather than as after-dinner drinks, should have the same treatment as sherry.

Opinions differ as to whether sweet sherries should be chilled or not. If they are to be presented as after-dinner wines, they should be uncooled but if used as aperitifs, they may be served as chilled wines or else 'on the rocks'. The ice treatment helps to give them a more acceptable lightness, partly on account of the cold and partly because the melting ice cubes help to dilute the wine. The same applies to other rich, fortified wines. Let them dally in the refrigerator or clunk with ice cubes. In both cases, ice cubes are better drinking.

Glasses need not be special. Hock and Moselle glasses – the ones made of coloured glass standing on long stems – are anachronisms. Silver-plated and even solid silver vessels have no place in the wine scene either, except for those who have a liking for wine that tastes of metal.

There is no need to have a great array of glasses of one kind or another. Those for light wines need only be the old Paris goblet, a thin-glassed vessel with a stem and base. The drinker holds the glass by the stem to keep the warmth of his hand away from the wine, which would otherwise change its temperature. Besides, cold or cooled wines are uncomfortable in the hand.

This is not to say that more stylish glasses should be banned. The main requirement of light wine glasses is that the glass should not be thick, so that the drinker can see the wine clearly, and that the glass should have a stem.

Glasses for sherry or port may be much more elaborate, fashioned, perhaps, in cut-glass, or in whatever shape may appeal. Champagne glasses should never be of the old saucer style, like a half melon. These are still shown on posters with bubbles leaping out of them, but they let too many bubbles escape within too short a period so that the wine falls flat too soon. The tall, skinny flute glass holds the bubbles and the flavour of the wine far better.

The notion of decanting, pouring wine from its bottle into another, sounds improbably fussy. But again, like the other guidelines for serving wine, it has its sensible points.

Wines to be decanted are mostly middle-aged to elderly reds. They contain a sediment of bits and pieces of grape which have not been dissolved into the wine. There is nothing unwholesome about them; a fine wine without sediment would be, to say the least, suspect. So the wine is poured from its original bottle into another vessel, leaving the sediment in the bottle. This may involve losing an inch or so of the original bottle's contents, but this residue – the sediment, plus the small quantity of wine in which the sediment is caught up – need not go down the sink. Use it in a casserole or stew a day or two later.

Apart from taking it off the sediment, the decanting process helps to give the wine some air, which will bring out its real character. Very old wines should be decanted only ten minutes or so before they are due to be poured into glasses, otherwise exposure to air will cause them to collapse and lose their character.

There are one or two other sensible guidelines worth following. Glasses, which should be of ample size though not ostentatiously so, should never be filled to the brim but only to about half to two-thirds of their capacity. This will enable the bouquet, an important attribute of good wine, to linger and help to contain it within the glass.

The order of serving is no less important. Wines need to ascend in importance, so that if an Alsatian Gewürztraminer is the aperitif or the first-course wine, then more stately wines should follow it. For instance, a higher-rated white should come next with, say, the fish course and a fine red then take over for the main part of the meal, followed by the best Sauternes available. In the case of a meal that is accompanied by a series of vintage reds, they should build up to a crescendo, from the youngest to the most elderly.

Wine as an Aperitif

Wines are the best of appetite sharpeners. By far the most popular wine for this purpose in Britain is sherry, and the ideal sherry styles for pre-prandial drinking are the drier ones, Fino and Manzanilla. The most popular, however, is the fuller Amontillado, which is usually partly sweet and the choice of those who find dry sherry too severe. The sweeter sherry styles are likely to be too rich to make good aperitifs, tending to dull the appetite rather than sharpen it.

A good, though usually more expensive, alternative to sherry is Madeira – a fortified wine, like sherry, but with a distinctly more assertive flavour. Again, the sweeter wines are too heavy to stimulate the appetite, but the drier versions, Sercial and Verdelho, make good and interesting aperitifs. Verdelho is less dry and could be roughly equated with the Amontillado style of sherry.

White and old Tawny ports are also good.

Then there is the extensive range of vermouths available on the UK market, from dry whites to sweet and fulsome reds. Each to his choice, for many people have a decided preference for sweet drinks, though the dry styles are unquestionably better suited to whet the appetite. One of the best dry vermouths – little heard of but fairly generally available – is Chambéry from the Savoie region of France. It has a good flavour of herbs, is light-bodied and not too dry. Nothing surpasses it as a prelude to a good meal.

Wine-based aperitifs abound, many of them of French origin, and many, therefore, sweet or sweetish, since this is the kind of drink that seems to work up appetites in France. Nowadays, though, there are sweet, semi-sweet or dry versions, all of them interesting and agreeable but without the thrust of alcohol that many spirit aperitifs have. Sold under brand names, the most notable of which are St-Raphaël and Dubonnet, they are round about the strength of sherry, and are pleasurable without being potent.

Sparkling wines, and Champagne in particular, give a lift to any special occasion. The dry styles of Champagne, labelled *extra dry*, *extra sec*, or *brut*, are the best for aperitif purposes. Many retailers have their own brands, usually priced at a figure below the best-known Champagne names. There are plenty of other sound sparkling wines on the market, lower in price than even the least expensive Champagnes. Examples include wines made by the Champagne method in Anjou, Saumur, Vouvray and Touraine; German wines (*sekt*) from the Rhine and Mosel; and the Italian Asti Spumante, though this is likely to appeal to those with sweeter tastes.

Red wines are not normally taken as aperitifs, but just about any wholesome white wine that is not decisively sweet will serve extremely well as an aperitif, though some are more suitable than others. There are whites from sun-baked regions, for example, with a scorched, earthy flavour that comes over too vigorously when there is no well-flavoured food to subdue it. At the other end of the scale there are sun-starved, underweight whites which will be too lean in flavour and probably too acidic to make completely agreeable pre-prandial drinking. In between these two extremities, however, is a whole battalion of bottles which will perform successfully as aperitifs and which can, if called on to do so, run along just as well with the meal to follow.

Very dry white wines are widely regarded as the best aperitifs. Among them are wines made from the Sylvaner grape in Alsace and Germany.

From France come Sancerre, Muscadet, Pouilly-Blanc-Fumé, Chablis, and Bourgogne Aligoté, and there are whites from north Italy.

It is a mistake, however, to choose only completely dry wines for party guests. Many people find even the finest of them to be sour. Wine which is soft and supple and which may have some discreet sweetness is more likely to be unanimously acceptable.

The most suitable wines with some or all of these characteristics come mostly from the better-rated wine regions and are not likely to be in the budget-bottle category. All the same, white wine as an aperitif is not likely to be any more costly than other kinds of aperitif, and will certainly be less expensive than spirits plus mixers.

There is something to be said for choosing middle-class rather than top-class wines for aperitif purposes. If a different wine is going to be served with the meal, irrespective of whether it is red, white or rosé, it ought to be of a better quality than the wine that has preceded it.

Vouvray, from the Loire, is one of the best of aperitif wines. It can be dry or semi-dry or even, in an exceptional vintage, markedly sweet. The middle-of-the-road demi-sec will have a good dry start with a slightly honeyed edge in its after-taste. Because it comes in *sec* and *demi-sec* versions, Vouvray is one of the best offerings that France has in the way of an all-round aperitif wine. But there are scores of others. Bordeaux, for example, offers sound whites at fairly light-weight prices.

Avoid the confectionery end of the French whites, such as Sauternes, Barsac, and Monbazillac. They will be too sweet. Any wine merchant should be able to come up with a well-fruited dry or semi-dry white wine with the Bordeaux appellation.

Many German wines make attractive drinking as aperitifs. In general, Rhines and Moselles from the *Qualitätswein* grade may be more suitable than the usually more costly wines with a special distinction like Spätlese or Auslese. These wines, made from late-gathered, selected grapes, can often be too ripe in flavour to succeed in sharpening the appetite.

German wines are a good choice for those who want to buy large-sized bottles. *Tafelwein*, the lowest grade, is more likely to be an agreeable wine than anything in economy-size containers from other wine-producing countries. There is virtually no end to the choice of aperitif-style wines from Germany, and any merchant should be able to recommend something suitable.

Rosé wine can also make an acceptable aperitif,

particularly in warm weather when the pink colouring has a way of catching the spirit of the season. There are firm, well-flavoured dry rosés from Tavel, in southern France, and other good rosés are made in Provence, Bordeaux, Loire valley and elsewhere in France. Most wine-producing countries make rosé: a good Italian one is Chiaretto, from Lake Garda, and Hungarian rosé can offer remarkably good value.

Wine and Food

Red Beaujolais with salmon, Sauternes with Roquefort and vintage Champagne with roast lamb are some of the less common wine and food pairings that may be encountered. Though unusual, they are not all that outrageous, despite the old familiar rules that prescribe white wine with fish or white meat and red with red meat or cheese. There is no rule about wine and food that does not have its exceptions. In regions producing mainly white wine, that is likely to be the wine taken with food of any kind and red is the wine most often drunk in red wine regions. Even in Britain, a couple of hundred years ago, white wine was likely to be the only wine served at any meal, red being considered rather vulgar, to be quaffed by the men after the ladies had withdrawn.

But the established rules have plenty of sensible points. Anyone who has ventured to try a red Burgundy with oysters will certainly appreciate why Chablis or Muscadet are, by general assent, considered more suitable. The order of wine and food generally accepted in the UK is designed for lunch or dinner-party planners who are likely to want to keep to the conventional combinations rather than visit their individual preferences upon guests.

Appetites and purses have become leaner since the days of the Edwardians, who would scoff their way through seven or more courses with a different wine at each course. A wine to accompany soup is now considered an extravagance if it is considered at all, while dessert wines, in their original role as accompaniments to the dessert rather than following it, away from the table, are out of fashion.

Still, a wine at each course in a three-course meal is an engaging thought for a special-occasion dinner party and it need not be excessively expensive. With a bit of luck, guests who know that there is the prospect of plenty of wine with their dinner will go easy on the aperitifs, so that total expenditure on drinks may even out.

Most hosts, however, will want to have one, or at the most two, wines with a meal. The following suggestions are designed for those who want to choose wines for anything from a simple picnic to a meal on a majestic scale.

SOUP Since wine has nothing to give to vegetable or fish soups, it is better to abstain. Thick meat soups can be on good terms with Amontillado or Fino sherry, with a dry or medium Montilla, or with Verdelho or Sercial Maderia. Consommé based on a meat stock can be enhanced by dry sherry or Sercial Maderia.

FISH Nothing should be served with prawn cocktail. Chablis, Muscadet, dry white Bordeaux, Alsatian, Austrian, Frascati, Soave, or a host of other dry whites go well with smoked fish, oysters, crayfish, unsauced prawns, whelks and mussels. Plainly prepared white fish can also be accompanied by any of these, or else by a white wine with a trace of sweetness to it, such as hock or one of the inexpensive Riesling wines from Eastern or Central Europe. Fish served with a thick cheese or anchovy sauce is likely to be on better terms with such wines than with the drier varieties.

PASTA, RICE A straightforward cheesy pasta needs a straightforward white wine, such as

Orvieto or Soave, whereas a very creamy pasta might be happier with the sweetish version of Orvieto, known as *abboccato* or *amabile*. Pasta or risotto with a dominant flavour of anchovy or prawns needs a dry Orvieto, Soave or Frascati. And meaty, substantial pastas will want a robust red – anything from Barbera to the stately Barolo, depending on the occasion and the fullness of flavour of the dish.

ROAST BEEF, STEAKS, LAMB The best choice would be claret, Burgundy, Rhône, or any sound red wine that has sufficient body to strike an accord with well-flavoured meat.

VEAL, PORK Either red or white wine would be suitable depending on the assertiveness of the accompaniments. With unassertive trimmings a dry white Bordeaux with good body is a sound choice; if there are thrustful vegetable flavours, like leeks or artichokes, go for a lightweight red such as Valpolicella or Bardolino. Alternatively, a fairly light-bodied Beaujolais would be very agreeable.

CHICKEN, TURKEY Much depends on what the trimmings are. A plain roast chicken will have a good accord with a light dry or dryish white wine. Examples are Vouvray, Touraine, Soave, Hungarian Riesling and Moselle. Chicken or turkey served with a variety of well-flavoured trimmings, such as sage and onion or chestnut stuffing, can be handsomely complemented by Beaujolais.

GOOSE, DUCK Birds with a distinctive flavour need a distinctively flavoured wine. For these two birds it could be a well-flavoured white or a moderately flavoured red. In the former category come the dry styles of white Bordeaux and Rheingau wines, with a margin of sweetness. Beaujolais, Valpolicella or the firm dry rosés of Tavel or Provence could fit equally well.

COLD MEATS The traditional post-Christmas assortment of turkey and ham calls for a light red, and Beaujolais is a prime choice. Cold meats served in summer will be just as happy with the same wine, cooled, or with a dry to dryish white such as Orvieto. Cold beef, however, will want a red with a deep flavour; claret fits the bill, but not a pricey one. Cold food seldom brings out the best in good red wines.

GAME, CASSEROLES Big, sun-warmed reds are the only wines for these dishes. They take up the warmth of the food in their great glowing full-ness. For some dishes, like venison, choose a solid red Burgundy or a full, fruity claret. Casseroles deserve the same style of wine, though perhaps one rather less pricey, like Châteauneuf du Pape or Côtes du Rhône. But any well-bodied and embracing wine will fit in admirably. Try Hungary's Bull's Blood, a wine to measure up to goulash or comparable spicy casseroles, or the voluptuous reds of Italy, like Barolo or Barbaresco. In short, choose anything red that has fullness and ember-warmth in it.

CHEESE No wine should be served with cream cheese or Camembert. Most English cheeses are handsomely complemented by virtually any kind of red wine, but strong blue cheeses are likely to swamp the flavour of even the sturdiest red, though they are good with port. There is no need to consider a special wine for the cheese course. In France, the cheese is served before the pudding so that the red wine left over from the main course can be used up.

PUDDINGS, FRUIT Sauternes is the classic wine at this stage of the meal and the finer it is, the more luscious and successful it will be. Cheap Sauternes is sweet, but can be disappointingly thin. Tokay

and the German Beerenauslese and Trockenbeerenauslese are other fine sweet wines; sweet
Champagne is a good choice, with Asti Spumante
as a cheaper alternative. All go well with lighter
puddings and with ripe fruit, especially peaches
and pears. Darker flavoured puddings need a
darker flavoured wine, which may be a Cream
sherry, a Malmsey, Bual Madeira or Marsala.
Any pudding with tart ingredients – oranges, for
instance, lemons or rhubarb will not be enhanced
by wine, nor will those made of chocolate or ice
cream.

Wine after a Meal

Port is the traditional after-dinner wine. Vintage
port is the finest but it needs careful decanting and
must have sufficient age – a minimum of eight
years after the vintage date, and preferably more.
A good and less expensive alternative is Late-
bottled port, which goes through its ageing
process in cask, is ready for instant drinking and
needs no decanting. Cheaper than either of these is
Ruby, the plainest and youngest port style there
is. Tawny port is better than Ruby, having been
aged in cask, so losing its ruby colour and
acquiring considerable softness and a good nutty
flavour.

The sweeter styles of Madeira also make good post-prandial drinking. These are Bual, which is a golden, honeyed wine, and the more luscious, deeply flavoured Malmsey.

Sherry is regarded as an aperitif wine but the sweet versions are at their best at the end of a meal. The sweetest are Oloroso, Cream and Brown. Dry Oloroso is occasionally encountered but it would be out of place as an after-dinner drink.

Other sweet, dark wines which can have a place after a meal include Marsala and Malaga.

In the Restaurant

Restaurants impose a tremendous mark-up on their wines. They have been invited not to do so, but for the most part persist. They like to see wine sales as a considerably greater contributor to their profits than food. There is very little to be done about it, except for public vilification or, better still, scorn. Scorn is what the restaurateur most abhors.

Restaurants are now tending to list their wines under country or regional headings. This helps to clear some the headaches created when lists simply sectionalized wines into sparkling, red, white and (occasionally) rosé.

The practice of placing an 'also ran' wine as number two on the list, or a section of the list, persists despite exposure. The theory is that the customer will avoid number one which is, traditionally, the cheapest wine shown and, not wishing to pay too much beyond his means, will opt for the second cheapest, number two. Always look at number two carefully.

There are restaurants which will attempt to offload poor or indifferent vintages on to customers. These wines can be bought fairly cheaply but are unlikely to be sold cheaply in the restaurant. The customer with a vintage chart in his pocket will be able to judge their value for himself.

Traditionally, in a restaurant the waiter will pour a small quantity of wine into the host's glass for him to taste. Never turn down the opportunity. Some restaurants keep their wines indifferently, if not badly, and while the chances of coming across an 'off' wine are fairly slender, such wines do turn up.

If in doubt about its condition, send the wine back. 'Faults in Wine' (page 20) explains what to look for. It is unlikely that the restaurant manager, however stony-faced he may seem at the outset, will ultimately refuse to take a faulty wine away and replace it with another. He, in turn, can send it back to the supplier or possibly it will go into tomorrow's *coq au vin*.

The contents of a restaurant's carafe wine is controlled by law. It is obligatory to sell carafes of wine in stipulated quantities: 25 cl, 50 cl, 75 cl and one litre, and 10 fl oz or 20 fl oz. The quantities of carafes must be displayed on the premises.

Ordinary waiters are not likely to be able to advise on wine, though head waiters and managers may be able to do so. Some restaurants, however, have a waiter called the sommelier who specializes in wine. He can be expected to know his stuff, especially if he is a member of the Guild of Sommeliers.

Glossary of
Tasting Terms

This glossary lists English terms that are commonly used in appraising wines. They are taster's terms; the majority are unlikely to appear on labels or lists and, naturally, the derogatory terms will not appear there at all.

Wine connoisseurs and compilers of wine lists are likely to have their own lexicon of descriptive terms, but in general they are only variations of the more commonly used words listed here.

French, German and Italian label words of description indicating that the wine in the bottle is sweet, medium, dry or sparkling are listed separately in the dictionary.

ACETIC Smelling or tasting of vinegar. This is usually the result of faulty fermentation or bottling.

ACID, ACIDIC Acid is a necessary component of wine, but those with acid showing too prominently are unbalanced. In young wines the condition passes with time.

AFTER-TASTE The lingering presence of the flavour of wine in the mouth. This is usually an agreeable sensation and indicative of a good wine.

AROMA The grapey smell of a wine. It develops into a bouquet as the wine itself develops.

ASTRINGENT Sharp, unfriendly on the palate. A condition that is common among wines that are too young to drink, especially those with high acidity. Astringent wines can become mellow with age.

BALANCE The relationship between the components of a wine. A well-balanced wine is one in which all the components have come together in complete harmony. It will not necessarily be a great wine, but it will be a good one.

BIG An amply flavoured wine, often, though not necessarily, with a high alcoholic strength. This term is usually applied to red wines.

BITTER Generally suggestive of a fault, especially in mature wine. Bitterness can be imparted by casks that are out of condition.

BODY The weight that a wine has on the palate. Full-bodied is akin to big, among reds, but white and rosé wines can have good body.

BONE DRY A wine in which no sweetness is present.

BOUQUET The complete scent of a mature wine. Some wines have little bouquet, but can be well flavoured. A good bouquet, however, is an important attribute in a wine.

BREED Wine of an elegant style, having been made from good grapes grown in a prime location, and carefully vinified.

CHARACTER A wine of any style which has a positive, distinctive personality.

CLEAN A term which is most commonly applied to

white wine. It means pure on the palate and the nose.

COARSE Wine lacking refinement, rough. Such wines are generally the result of careless vinification.

COMMON Plain wine, though not necessarily of low quality. It denotes wine of no special distinction.

CORKY A condition that develops when the cork disintegrates, releasing particles of decaying cork into the wine. When poured, a wine so affected will be cloudy, and will give off an unpleasant, musty odour.

CRISP Dry, refreshing. The term is usually applied to white wines with a good proportion of acidity.

DEPTH Term applied, usually to red wine, to indicate a deep flavour. Good clarets, for example, should be expected to have some depth.

DELICATE A gently flavoured wine, mostly applied to white wines but sometimes to reds. In general delicate wines will not keep for very long.

DRY A wine without sweetness, but not so totally dry as to be rated bone dry. But in the case of sherry, on the UK market, dry can sometimes prove to be a wine that is not markedly sweet.

EARTHY A wine that has taken on, in its flavour and bouquet, some of the characteristics of the soil in which the vine was grown. Many of the wines described as earthy come from vineyards with a hot climate, where the warmth of the sun throws something of the character of the soil back into the vine and its grapes.

FAT Full-bodied, but unbalanced as a result of shortage of acidity. Substantially flavoured, but it will lack firmness.

FINE There is no definition of a fine wine, but the word

is usually reserved for the better growths of Bordeaux, Burgundy, and certain important areas of Germany.

FINESSE A wine with great style, breeding, and distinction. This is one of the greatest words of praise.

FRESH Comparable with light-bodied, dry. This will apply to a wine with an acceptably high level of acidity, normally used to describe dry white wines, but sometimes dry, light-bodied reds and occasionally rosés.

FLABBY Much the same as fat; lacking acidity, though having a full flavour. Such a wine will lack 'bite'.

FLAT Primarily, a sparkling wine that has lost its sparkle, but the term is also used to describe non-sparkling wines that for one reason or another (oxidization is not the least of them) have become dull in bouquet, flavour and general impact.

FLINTY The dry, clean, hard taste of certain white wines, reminiscent of the smell of gun flint. Wines with this characteristic are well rated, and include Pouilly-Blanc-Fumé and some wines from the Chablis district of Burgundy.

FLOWERY The scent of spring flowers that can be detected in the bouquet of some of the best white wines, and sometimes in reds. German wines made from the Riesling grape, or versions of it, are a notable example.

FRUITY A wine that smells strongly of fruit, not just grapes but raspberries, plums or blackberries.

GRAPEY A wine with a strong flavour of grapes. This is most pronounced among wines made from the Muscat grape, but often present in wines pressed from any other distinctively flavoured grape.

HARD As a general description for a wine, hard is a

derogatory term, probably indicating an excess of tannin. Such wines make indifferent drinking, but as a general rule they will become softer as they acquire bottle age.

HEARTY Wines that deserve this description are usually red, with a warm, generous flavour, and maybe with a high level of alcohol. Red wines from the Rhône valley and Algeria are among examples.

HEAVY Red or white wines with a sultry flavour; full-bodied wines lacking finesse. The term is also used to describe wines that are heavy in alcoholic strength.

LIGHT Strictly, an EEC wine definition, but in tasting terms a wine of slender body and probably low in alcoholic strength. The term is not a derogatory one and light wines, red or white, are especially suitable for warm-weather drinking.

LIVELY Sometimes applied to young, fresh, sprightly white wines, but the more common usage relates to wines that have a slight sparkle, or natural petillance.

MADEIRIZED White wine that has passed its peak, and takes on a flavour of old age. It becomes tinged with brown, and smells of Madeira. Such wines can be consumed, but they may prove to be unpalatable.

MEDIUM Neither sweet nor dry. The perfect medium wine is exactly what it suggests it should be: halfway between sweet and dry. Few are, wavering between one extreme and the other. The only sure thing to be said for a medium wine is that it will not be exceedingly sweet or exceedingly dry. Among sherries the matter is especially complicated, with wines sold under brand names embracing the word 'dry' that prove to be distinctly on the sweet side. For lack of definition, the only course is to sample.

MELLOW A state reached by wine when it has become round and amenable with age. Normally this is applied to reds. The rough edges have worn off, and the wine is ready to drink. Some reds can achieve mellowness but can continue to become more and more mellow with bottle age. The term is not synonymous with softness, which may be a feature of a mellow wine but is not necessarily so.

MUSTY A smell that can come from any wine of any quality. If it is confined to the cork and capsule, it is likely that the wine inside the bottle will be perfectly drinkable. If the wine itself gives off a musty odour, this may pass if it is decanted for two or three hours. Should the smell persist after that, the likely indication is that the wine is ailing and is not fit for consumption.

NOSE The olfactory sensation provided by a wine. Even before tasting it can give an indication of the style and status of the wine, which should be gently swirled in the glass to release its bouquet.

NUTTY A term applied most frequently to sherries or to red wines, which can sometimes release an aroma reminiscent of walnuts or hazel nuts. The smell indicates a good, wholesome, well-flavoured wine which will be a pleasure to drink.

OXIDIZED A lamentable condition for any wine. It means that the wine has been exposed to air, perhaps during the bottling process or possibly because the cork does not fit. The general symptoms are a bad smell and, in the case of white or rosé wines, a darkening of the colour. There is no remedy; the bottle must go back to the retailer.

PERFUME Similar to bouquet, but usually associated with wines pressed from grapes which are characteristically 'perfumed', such as the Muscat. But some inferior wines are deliberately blended with sweet-smelling grapes to give them a good 'nose'. An agreeable perfume on the nose is never an indication of a good wine.

PIQUANT The flavour of a wine, usually white, that has a higher degree of acidity than others, giving it an agreeably sharp flavour. Piquant wines of the best kind come from certain areas of the Rhine, Mosel and Loire.

RICH This term can apply to big red wines or sweet white wines. Among reds it means a handsomely flavoured wine; describing sweet wines it means simply 'sweet'. The word is also used by producers in the Champagne region of France to indicate the sweetest of their wines.

RIPE A condition reached by a wine when it is completely mature. After this stage it may well start to decline.

ROBUST A sturdy wine, though not necessarily a tough one. The word means stout-hearted, long-lasting. It is invariably reserved for red wine.

ROUGH Very plain wine, unlikely to be encountered in Britain. It will probably not achieve the standards of French *ordinaire*.

ROUND A state approaching near-perfection, attained by a red wine from a good vintage that has spent several years in bottle. A round wine is one that, while not necessarily fine, is easy and pleasing to the palate.

SEVERE A sharp wine, one that is not far short of astringent. Most likely such a wine is immature and highly acidic, but will become mellower if kept in bottle for a time.

SHARP Akin to 'severe', but probably not so decisively sour on the palate. Sharp wines may be immature, but they may equally be wines that are deliberately made sharp, being vinified from grapes that are barely ripe. Others may come from an indifferent vintage, pressed from grapes that have not reached the right stage of maturity.

SHORT Wine that is short on flavour, and probably on bouquet, too. Such a wine may have an immediate, positive flavour at the first mouthful, but has no depth or character.

SILKY Relates to the texture of a wine on the palate; almost always applied to red wines with good bottle age. A superlative term.

SMOOTH A wine that makes amiable drinking, largely on account of its texture. Such a wine will have an abundance of soft, mellow flavour.

SOFT Usually a statement about the impact of a red wine on the palate. Soft wines are not necessarily smooth or mellow; relatively young wines can be soft. Much depends on the grape variety they are pressed from.

SOUR Wine that is either too young to drink and may improve, or one from a poor vintage, which is not likely to improve significantly.

SPICY A few grape varieties make wines that can be

so described. The most important. of them is the Gewürztraminer, especially when it is grown in the Alsace region of France. Such wines have a distinct flavour of herbs as well as of spices.

STALKY Some wine makers leave the grape stalks in contact with the pressed grapes for too long. This can impart an unpleasant taste of damp twigs to the wine. This is not likely to happen at the great châteaux of France, or at other large vineyards where the vinification process is carefully supervised, but it may occur at lesser properties where proper procedures are not always strictly followed.

SULPHURY Sulphur is used as a preservative in wine, but sometimes the producer can overdo the dose. The result is a wine that has a pungent smell of sulphur. It may clear after half an hour or so; if not, the offending bottle will have to be returned to the retailer.

SUPPLE An attribute of any kind of wine, from the great growths down to the most humble, that is pliable and amenable on the palate. The term is most usually used in connection with reds.

SWEET A term usually applied to white wines, but sometimes to reds, with a discernible sweetness in them. Mostly they are made from sweet grapes that are allowed to ripen in the sun, thereby increasing their concentration of sugar.

TANNIC Tannin is a group of organic substances in the pips, the skins and the stalks of grapes. It is one of the components that must be tempered and softened as a red wine matures. Tannic wine is one that has not achieved this transformation; it will taste hard and disagreeable.

Tannin takes some years to marry into the body of the wine, which is why it is important to buy red wines that are fully mature, unless they are intended for laying down.

TART Very sharp. This is an undesirable condition mainly to be found in wine that is too young and needs time to soften, or in wine made from under-ripe grapes.

THIN A wine lacking in body and flavour; insipid, watery.

VELVETY Very smooth, softly textured. The term is applied to the feel of a wine on the tongue, not to its flavour.

VINOSITY A property of any wine that meets generally acceptable standards and has good, balanced wine-style characteristics.

WEIGHTY Wine of depth and character, usually applied to full-bodied reds.

WOODY A flavour of wood which, if it is marked, will make a wine disagreeable. It can be the result of an over-long period in cask, or of some fault in the cask.

YEASTY A smell of yeast that suggests a secondary fermentation has taken place, or is about to do so.

Classification of French Wines

In 1855, the wines of two of the leading districts of Bordeaux were placed in a 'league' of five divisions. The original classification remains a dependable pointer to the merit of the classified châteaux. (See also **classifications**, page 113).

Médoc Classification of 1855

CHÂTEAUX   DISTRICT

Premiers Crus

Château Lafite	Pauillac
Château Margaux	Margaux
Château Latour	Pauillac
Château Mouton–Rothschild	Pauillac
Château Haut–Brion	Pessac (Graves)

Deuxièmes Crus

Château Rausan–Ségla	Margaux
Château Rauzan–Gassies	Margaux
Château Léoville Las Cases	Saint-Julien
Château Léoville Poyferré	Saint-Julien
Château Léoville–Barton	Saint-Julien
Château Durfort–Vivens	Margaux
Château Lascombes	Margaux
Château Gruaud–Larose	Saint-Julien
Château Brane–Cantenac	Cantenac
Château Pichon-Longueville-Baron	Pauillac
Château Pichon-Lalande	Pauillac

Château Ducru-Beaucaillou — Saint-Julien
Château Cos d'Estournel — Saint-Estèphe
Château Montrose — Saint-Estèphe

Troisièmes Crus

Château Kirwan — Cantenac
Château d'Issan — Cantenac
Château Lagrange — Saint-Julien
Château Langoa-Barton — Saint-Julien
Château Giscours — Labarde
Château Malescot-Saint-Exupéry — Margaux
Château Cantenac-Brown — Cantenac
Château Palmer — Cantenac
Château la Lagune — Ludon
Château Desmirail — Margaux
Château Calon-Ségur — Saint-Estèphe
Château Ferrière — Margaux
Château Marquis d'Alesme — Margaux
Château Boyd-Cantenac — Margaux

Quatrièmes Crus

Château Saint-Pierre-Sevaistre — Saint-Julien
Château Branaire — Saint-Julien
Château Talbot — Saint-Julien
Château Duhart-Milon-Rothschild — Pauillac
Château Pouget — Cantenac
Château La Tour-Carnet — Saint-Laurent
Château Lafon-Rochet — Saint-Estèphe
Château Beychevelle — Saint-Julien
Château Prieuré-Lichine — Cantenac
Château Marquis-de-Terme — Margaux

Cinquièmes Crus

Château Pontet-Canet — Pauillac
Château Batailley — Pauillac
Château Haut-Batailley — Pauillac

Château Grand-Puy-Lacoste	Pauillac
Château Grand-Puy-Ducasse	Pauillac
Château Lynch-Bages	Pauillac
Château Lynch-Moussas	Pauillac
Château Dauzac-Lynch	Labarde
Château Mouton-d'Armailhacq (now Mouton-Baronne-Philippe)	Pauillac
Château du Tertre	Arsac
Château Haut-Bages-Libéral	Pauillac
Château Pédesclaux	Pauillac
Château Belgrave	Saint-Laurent
Château Camensac	Saint-Laurent
Château Cos-Labory	Saint-Estèphe
Château Clerc-Milon	Pauillac
Château Croizet-Bages	Pauillac
Château Cantemerle	Macau

Sauternes Classification of 1855

CHÂTEAUX	DISTRICT
Premier Grand Cru	
Château d'Yquem	Sauternes
Premiers Crus	
Château La Tour-Blanche	Bommes
Château Lafaurie-Peyraguey	Bommes
Clos Haut-Peyraguey	Bommes
Château de Rayne-Vigneau	Bommes
Château de Suduiraut	Preignac
Château Coutet	Barsac
Château Climens	Barsac
Château Guïraud	Sauternes
Château Rieussec	Fargues
Château Rabaud-Promis	Bommes
Château Sigalas-Rabaud	Bommes

Deuxièmes Crus

Château Doisy-Daëne	Barsac
Château Doisy-Védrines	Barsac
Château d'Arche	Sauternes
Château Filhot	Sauternes
Château Broustet	Barsac
Château Caillou	Barsac
Château Suau	Barsac
Château de Malle	Preignac
Château Romer	Fargues
Château Lamothe	Sauternes
Château Nairac	Barsac

St-Émilion Classification of 1955

The best red wines of St-Émilion were classified in 1955 by the French Institut National des Appellations d'Origine. These are the First Great Growths though the classification also lists some 70 Great Growths.

First Great Growths
(Premiers Grands Crus Classés)

Château Ausone
Château Cheval-Blanc
Château Beauséjour-Duffau-Lagarrosse
Château Beauséjour-Bécot
Château Bel-Air
Château Canon
Château Figeac
Château La Gaffelière
Château La Magdelaine
Château Pavie
Château Trottevieille
Clos Fourtet

67

Graves Classification of 1959

The Graves vineyards were officially classified by the Institut National des Appellations d'Origine in 1953. The classification was revised in 1959.

CHÂTEAUX   DISTRICT

Graves Classified Red Wines
(Crus Classés Rouges)

Château Bouscaut	Cadaujac
Château Haut-Bailly	Léognan
Château Carbonnieux	Léognan
Domaine de Chevalier	Léognan
Château Fieuzal	Léognan
Château Olivier	Léognan
Château Malartic-Lagravière	Léognan
Château Latour-Martillac	Martillac
Château Smith-Haut-Lafitte	Martillac
Château Haut-Brion	Pessac
Château La Mission-Haut-Brion	Pessac
Château Latour-Haut-Brion	Talence

Graves Classified White wines
(Crus Classés Blancs)

Château Bouscaut	Cadaujac
Château Carbonnieux	Léognan
Domaine de Chevalier	Léognan
Château Malartic-Lagravière	Léognan
Château Olivier	Léognan
Château La Tour-Martillac	Martillac
Château Laville-Haut-Brion	Talence
Château Couhins	Villenave-d'Ornon

Dictionary of Wines

*The wines described in this
book are those which are fairly readily
available in Britain, and do not therefore
represent a fully comprehensive
list of world wines.*

AC *(France)* see **Appellation d'Origine Contrôlée**

ageing Bringing wines to maturity. There are usually two stages. The first is in the hands of the producer, who devotes a good deal of his cellar space to ageing wines in cask; the second is in the hands of the purchaser, whether merchant or consumer, who ages the wine further in bottle. Certain countries have laws which specify the minimum age at which a wine may be released. However, not all wines benefit by this treatment and some cheap wines will deteriorate after only a few months in bottle. Wines most likely to improve with ageing are Vintage port and certain full-bodied reds. See **laying down**.

Aigle Good, dry white Swiss wine made from

the Chasselas or Fendant grape in the canton of Vaud.

Aleatico *(Italy)* Grape variety, a member of the Muscat family. It produces red dessert wines in Tuscany, Puglia and elsewhere.

Alella *(Spain)* A good white wine from the village of Alella, north of Barcelona. It is usually semi-sweet.

Algeria *(North Africa)* Large producer of light wines, principally red. White and rosé wines are also produced but are of little significance in the UK. The wine industry of Algeria has been in the doldrums since the departure of large numbers of French wine growers, but the country continues to make good, full-bodied red wines which are available on the UK market. For the most part, they are labelled 'Algerian red wine' and district names are therefore of little consequence even if they should be shown on the label. However, the best qualities are grown on the relatively cool slopes of the Atlas mountains.

Aligoté A prolific grape variety, extensively cultivated in Burgundy, France, but even in these distinguished vineyards the wine it produces is not outstanding. Wine produced in Burgundy from the Aligoté grape will indicate its primary source and its place of origin, Bourgogne Aligoté.

Aloxe-Corton *(France)* A famous commune in the Côte de Beaune with a high reputation for white and red wines. The greatest white wine vineyard is Corton Charlemagne which makes, in small quantities, a big, rich, dry wine, strong in alcohol and with a superb nutty flavour. Distinguished red wine properties include Le Corton, Corton-Clos du Roi and Corton Les Bressandes. Lesser wines of the commune are often labelled Aloxe-Corton; the finer wines omit the prefix.

Alsace *(France)* Northernmost French wine region, running from Mulhouse to Strasbourg with the River Rhine some 15 miles to the east. The production is nearly all white, although some rosé is made. The region traditionally names its wines after the grape variety they are pressed from, rather than the district or parish name; some vineyards also use a brand name. The principal grapes are the Riesling, Gewürztraminer, Pinot Gris (known here as Tokay d'Alsace), Pinot Blanc, Sylvaner, Muscat, and Chasselas.

Rieslings, firm and fruity, are generally the

finest of the wines of Alsace, closely followed by
the spicy Gewürztraminer. Sylvaner is a light,
thirst-quenching wine, agreeably fruity. The
Muscat, not to be confused with the grape that
makes a sweet, perfumed wine elsewhere, produces good, dry wines with an emphatic bouquet.
Tokay d'Alsace is a dry, light, earthy wine. The
rosés are of no special merit.

Plainer blends are called Zwicker and blends
made from the better grape varieties are known as
Edelzwicker. Colmar is the centre of the wine
industry and other important placenames include
Ribeauvillé and Riquewihr. More important than
placenames in this region, however, are the names
of producers and among those of note are Dopff
and Irion, Hugel, Trimbach and Beyer. Wines
made from late-gathered and specially selected
grapes are described as *vendange tardive*, and may
be labelled 'Réserve Exceptionelle' or 'Grande
Réserve' to indicate superior quality.

The wines of Alsace are shipped in slender
green bottles of the kind used by Moselle producers.

Alto Douro *(Portugal)* The area of the valley of
the Douro river where port is produced.

amabile *(Italy)* A sweet or sweetish taste which

is pleasant or agreeable in the mouth. Normally this term is applied to wines that are more usually dry.

Amarone *(Italy)* Wine made from late-gathered grapes, notably in the Piedmont and Veneto regions. The grapes are given an additional drying-out period after being gathered. Red wines falling into this category are solid and full bodied and can develop magnificently in bottle.

Amontillado *(Spain)* Strictly a Fino sherry which has been aged in cask until it has acquired a round, soft and deep flavour. True Amontillado produced in this way is always dry. Today, because much sherry sold as Amontillado is not old Fino but a blend with added sweetness to suit the market, the name has become inextricably associated with a 'medium' sherry style.

Ämtliche Prüfungsnummer *(Germany)* Important piece of German wine labelling, usually condensed to AP Nr or just AP. The figures appearing after AP Nr show, among other things, the grade of the wine, the numbered vineyard of origin and the year in which it was bottled. These numbers appear only on wines of *Qualitätswein* standard or above; they will not be shown on wines in the *Tafelwein* or *Deutscher Tafelwein* grades.

Anbaugebiete *(Germany)* An officially recognized wine-producing region under German wine law. There are eleven such regions. The word is sometimes abbreviated to Gebiet.

Andalucia *(Spain)* Fertile region of Southern Spain, famous as the home of the sherry industry which is based on the city of Jerez, of which the word sherry is a corruption. Other good sherry-type wines are produced in Montilla and Huelva, and Malaga is notable for its dark brown dessert wine.

Anjou *(France)* Vineyards of this province run along both sides of the River Loire, and produce a wide variety of red, white and rosé wines. In the UK, Anjou Rosé is the best-known style; a pale pink, unassertive wine which is rather on the sweet side. Better, slightly more expensive wines of a drier style are made from the Cabernet grape. The whites include very attractive sweet wines, such as Coteaux du Layon and Coteaux de la Loire.

AP see **Ämtliche Prüfungsnummer**

aperitif *(France)* Any drink taken before a meal to sharpen the appetite. The most preferred are the dry versions of Champagne, sherry and dry white port, but sweet aperitifs, selling under a brand name, have become popular in the UK. Examples are Dubonnet and St-Raphaël, while red and sweet, white and sweet or white and dry vermouths are increasingly popular. White wines, either dry or fairly dry, are also acceptable. Examples include Moselle, the drier styles of Rhine wine, Vouvray, Gewürztraminer, Soave, Frascati and other white wines that are not too heavy in acidity. Very dry white wine with considerable acidity may well prove to be disagreeable before food.

Appellation d'Origine Contrôlée (AC) *(France)* The term applied under a good, though not infallible, French law designed to protect the reputation and quality of wine. AC wines are the league leaders and must conform to a number of strict requirements. The law defines the area in which an AC wine may be produced, the varieties of vine which may be used, the minimum level of alcohol and the maximum yield of wine per acre. This last provision is to prevent over-prolific production which could result in a reduction in quality. The narrower the geographic location, the finer a wine should be; thus, a wine entitled to a Médoc AC classification will be good, but not as good as one entitled to the Superior Haut-Médoc AC.

A second category governed by similar requirements is VDQS – *Vins délimités de qualité supérieure*. These are good, sound wines, less famous than those awarded an AC, but generally representing good value for money. Some are of a better standard than wines with a very broad AC, Bordeaux for example.

The third league is *Vins de pays* – wines of the country – for which the legal requirements are no less strict than for the better categories, but less onerous in terms of quality.

Arbois *(France)* A section of the Jura area and one of the most notable. Red, white and rosé wines are made here, as well as the uncommon *Vins pailles* (straw wines) and *Vin jaune* (yellow wine). Apart from these two latter specialities, the most highly rated wine of Arbois is rosé, dry, full-bodied and satisfying, which has been compared with the famous rosés of Tavel. The rosé wine of Arbois has achieved a good reputation on the UK market.

Argentina A major producer in the world wine

league. Red wines predominate, with the Malbec the most widely cultivated vine, followed by other European varieties, chiefly French and Italian. Argentinian wines exported to the UK are principally the less fine varieties, but nevertheless provide good everyday drinking. The main vineyard areas are Mendoza and San Juan.

Arrosto, Vino da *(Italy)* A big, beefy red wine, having above-average quality.

Arsac *(France)* Commune of the Haut-Médoc, its wines are entitled to the Margaux appellation. The major property is the fifth-growth Château du Tertre.

Asti Spumante *(Italy)* Aromatic sparkling wine with a full flavour made in and around the town of Asti in Piedmont. It is rather sweet, and takes its full flavour and bouquet from the Muscat grape.

aszú *(Hungary)* Grapes gathered late and therefore containing a high concentration of sugar, which have been affected by 'noble rot'. Specially selected, they are used in the production of Tokay.

Australia A major producer of wines of virtually

every style, with vineyards in almost every state. Quality is generally high and owing to the equable climate, vintages show only marginal variations. All the vines are of European origin; unlike America, there are no indigenous vines. The main regions are South Australia, New South Wales and Victoria. Many single vineyards produce an extensive variety of styles, which may range from sweet red fortified wine to dry light whites. Of the fortified wines, the port styles are, in general, more successful than the sherry styles and include several good examples of Tawny.

As in other wine-producing countries where district and parish names are scarcely known in Europe, proprietary names are an important pointer to quality. These include Hardy, Edwards and Chaffey, McWilliam, Hamilton, Seppelt, Angove, Stoneyfell, Lindeman, Penfold, Gramp, Smith and Wynn. Among the better-known district names are Barossa, Coonawara and the Murray River in South Australia; Great Western, Mildura, Rutherglen/Corowa and Tahbilk in Victoria, and the Hunter Valley in New South Wales.

The wine industry of Australia is technically well advanced and poor wine is rare, but the country does not produce any wines that could fairly be described as great or fine. The wines do, however, represent reasonable value for money.

The long-established practice of borrowing European names – Australian Chablis, for example, Burgundy and Sauternes – is not permitted in EEC countries.

Auslese *(Germany)* A superior style of white wine made from grapes that have been gathered after the normal harvest time and specially selected by the pickers for their exceptional maturity. Such wines will be full-flavoured and sweet. In an outstanding year they will be sweet enough to be consumed as dessert wines. They are superior to Spätlese wines, and are always expensive. See also **Beerenauslese** and **Trockenbeerenauslese**.

Austria A significant producer of wines, over 86 per cent of which are white, the majority of them being light, fresh, dry and flowery. The most widely cultivated grape is the Grüner Veltliner which has some of the characteristics of the spicy Gewürztraminer. Others include the Riesling, Furmint and Sylvaner. In the right conditions wines with special qualities are produced, such as Spätlese, Beerenauslese and Trockenbeerenauslese. The last two are not always as luscious as their German counterparts, but are likely to be considerably less costly.

Important districts include Wachau, Burgenland and Styria and the best known placename is Gumpoldskirchen. Most Austrian wine on the UK market is sold under brand names in slender German-style bottles. Austrian red wine is of little consequence outside the country.

Ay *(France)* Town in the Marne Valley, a centre of the Champagne industry. The best-known Champagne producer here is Bollinger.

Badacsony *(Hungary)* Notable centre of wine production in the Balaton district.

Baden *(Germany)* One of the eleven officially designated wine regions, and the third largest in terms of vineyard area. The predominant grape variety is the Müller-Thurgau, which accounts for more than one third of vines cultivated, but a wide range of grape species is grown. This, with the extensive area covered by the vineyards of Baden, gives an extremely varied array of styles, flavours and qualities, so that no generalized label can be attached to the character of Baden wines. The best, however, come from the Kaiserstuhl and Ortenau districts.

Bad Kreuznach *(Germany)* Principal wine centre of the Nahe region. It has some of the best vineyards of the region, including Narrenkappe, Hinkelstein and Kahlenberg.

Balaton *(Hungary)* A vast lake surrounded by vineyards in which an extensive variety of grapes is produced. The Furmint grape yields Balatoni Furmint, a graceful, golden, dry wine and wine made from the Olasz Riesling is agreeably dry, clean tasting and fresh. Main centres are Badacsony, Balatonfüred, and Csopak. Wines from Badacsony (labelled Badacsonyi) are likely to be sweeter and have more substance than the others.

Bandol *(France)* One of the better districts of Provence making sturdy red wines, and some white and rosé. The district is best known in the UK for its reds, which are not only sturdy but are likely to be fairly high in alcohol. The general expectation of a red Bandol wine is that it should be reasonably well balanced, strong and inexpensive.

Banyuls *(France)* Heady, fortified dessert wine made around the village of Banyuls in the Languedoc-Roussillon area. With age it takes on a pronounced Madeira-like flavour.

Barbaresco *(Italy)* A notable red wine from

Piedmont, and a near neighbour of the more famous Barolo. Though made from the same grape, the Nebbiolo, it tends to fall a little short of the high standards attained by Barolo. Nevertheless, it is unquestionably one of Italy's best red wines and can develop well if given a few years in bottle.

Barbera *(Italy)* The red grape cultivated mainly in the Piedmont region and producing an agreeable, everyday wine of no particular distinction.

Bardolino *(Italy)* An agreeable, light red wine from around the village of Bardolino in Veneto. Not unlike a solid rosé, it needs to be consumed within three years from the vintage date.

Barolo *(Italy)* One of the greatest of Italian red wines from the village of Barolo in Piedmont. It is a big-bodied, powerful wine, made from the noble Nebbiolo grape. Barolo spends more than three years in cask and will certainly benefit by a further five years or more in bottle. It is said to be Italy's longest-lived wine.

Barsac *(France)* The largest producing area of the Sauternes district. It is entitled to its own appellation, and many producers use it in preference to that of Sauternes, to which they are also entitled. The style of the sweet white wines of Barsac is considered to be second only to that of the commune of Sauternes itself. Notable properties in the commune include Château Coutet and Château Climens.

Bas–Médoc *(France)* Northernmost part of the Bordeaux region of Médoc making some of the region's cheaper wines which are sold simply as 'Médoc'. None ranks as a fine wine, but many are of sound quality and can make agreeable drinking at a lower price than many wines from more closely defined districts elsewhere in the Médoc.

Beaujolais *(France)* Large area in the south of Burgundy famous for light, fruity and racy red wines. Not all the wines produced here deserve that reputation; there are considerable variations in style and quality. Some white wine is also produced but it is not of great commercial significance on the UK market, although some of it is of fine quality. The reds, pressed from the Gamay grape which reaches the peak of its performance in this area, are mostly for drinking while they are young and still fresh; some, such as Beaujolais Primeur and Beaujolais Nouveau, are consumed within months of the vintage. Certain of the best categories, however, can with advantage be laid down for several years to develop in bottle.

Nine communes are entitled to use their names along with the Beaujolais appellation: Chénas, Fleurie, Moulin à Vent, St Amour, Morgon, Juliénas, Chiroubles, Brouilly, and Côte de Brouilly and the finest vineyards are located in these communes. Wines of a quality rated above average may use the appellations Beaujolais Villages or Beaujolais Supérieur.

Beaujolais Blanc *(France)* A white wine from the Beaujolais area, produced only in limited quantities. It is a dry, fruity and thirst-quenching wine, to be consumed when it is young.

Beaujolais Primeur and Beaujolais Nouveau *(France)* Young red wines from the Beaujolais area. Beaujolais Primeur is released for sale at midnight on November 15th of each year. After December 15th of the same year, releases of wine to be offered as Beaujolais Primeur must cease, although such wine already released may continue to be offered until the end of January. In a good year it is a passable wine for quaffing, but frequently it can be sharp owing to its high level of acidity. It needs to be consumed at once, and certainly by the end of April following the year of its vinification, otherwise it will become stale. Beaujolais Nouveau is similar, but may be labelled and sold as such until the following vintage; it is generally a more acceptable wine than Beaujolais Primeur.

Beaujolais Supérieur *(France)* Blended red wine from the Beaujolais area. French law requires that it has an alcoholic strength higher than that required for plain Beaujolais, and it is likely to be of better quality. It is much on a par with Beaujolais Villages.

Beaujolais Villages *(France)* Red wine entitled to this appellation must be from any of 35 named villages in the Beaujolais area. In quality, it will be superior to wine entitled only to the simple Beaujolais appellation and slightly stronger, but it is not likely to attain the standard of wines from the nine communes which have the right to use their names as *appellations d'origine*. Beaujolais Villages wines follow the general style of the area's reds: light, fresh and fruity, to be consumed early.

Beaune *(France)* Centre of the Burgundy wine industry in the Côte de Beaune, with its own important vineyard sites. Most of the wine is red and the better vineyards have a reputation for making soft, fragrant wines. Among notable properties are Les Fèves, Les Grèves and Les Marconnets.

Beerenauslese *(Germany)* Superb sweet white wine made from grapes selected singly from bunches left so late on the vine that they are affected by 'noble rot' (German *Edelfäule*) and have a massive concentration of natural sugar and fruit flavour. This is fully reflected in the wines which are nectar-like dessert wines. Beerenauslese is made only in especially outstanding years and is therefore rare and expensive. There are, however, even rarer and still more expensive versions of wines made by such means. See **Trocken-beerenauslese** and **Eiswein**.

Bernkastel *(Germany)* Famous district of the Mosel with an even more famous vineyard, the Bernkasteler Doktor. The wines of the district have a distinctly nutty flavour, and in a good year those of the Bernkasteler Doktor vineyards have this in a better measure than most. Bernkasteler Doktor produces exceptional wines which are always highly priced. The other vineyards that can claim the Bernkastel name are inclined to capitalize on it.

bin ends Remnants of wine such as surplus stock or discontinued lines which a wine merchant wants to dispose of. They are usually sold at a price below the going rate for comparable wines.

Bingen *(Germany)* A major wine-producing area of the Rheinhessen region. Its wines are generally of high quality, many of them being on a par with those from the most renowned areas of the region. Important vineyards include Rosengarten and Kirchberg.

black wine Black is an adjectival projection of a very dark red wine. The 'black wine' of Cahors is an example, but new vinification processes there and in other areas once notable for the depth of colour and flavour of their wines have virtually eliminated wines of this description.

Blanc de Blancs *(France)* A white wine which has been pressed only from white grapes. It is meaningful in Champagne, where wines produced solely from the Chardonnay grape have a special delicacy, which appeals to some tastes, but is too light a wine for those accustomed to conventional Champagne, a mixture of white and black grapes. The term Blanc de Blancs has been borrowed by winemakers elsewhere, but since most already make their wines from white grapes, it has no significance.

Blanquette de Limoux *(France)* A sparkling white wine which is usually rather sweet from the Languedoc-Roussillon area. Blanquette is the name of the grape once used and Limoux is the name of the village.

Blaye *(France)* An area of Bordeaux, making red and white wines. Although Blaye lies opposite the Médoc on the other side of the Gironde, it has no wines of outstanding merit. It is, however, a source of relatively inexpensive varieties. The best is a red carrying the appellation Premières Côtes de Blaye. Some whites also carry this appellation but do not have a great deal to commend them.

blended wines Nearly all light wines are blends. The great châteaux of Bordeaux blend the produce of different grapes, while producers of more ordinary wines blend the produce of good and poor years, avoiding the peaks and the troughs and making a wine that is more or less consistent from year to year. Sometimes blends are made from the produce of two specific years, neither dramatically good nor exceptionally bad, and the producer will indicate this by showing both years on his label. But for the most part blends are confined to the lower orders of wine, cheap and cheerful, made not only from the produce of differing vintages, but also from disparate vineyards. They are popular and usually cheap.

Bocksbeutel *(Germany)* The traditional green flask-shaped glass bottle in which the wine producers of Franconia offer their wines. It is said to be a survival of the wine skin, made from and resembling the scrotum of a goat.

bodega *(Spain)* A wine store. The word is sometimes adapted to mean wine bar or wine shop.

Bommes *(France)* A sweet white wine producing commune of Sauternes with the right to use the Sauternes appellation. Within the boundaries of Bommes are six of the first growths of Sauternes; they include Château la Tour-Blanche, Château Sigalas-Rabaud and also Château Haut-Peyraguey.

Bordeaux *(France)* A major city, seaport and centre of one of the world's finest wine regions, famed for red and white wines alike. Despite the renown of claret, as the red wine of Bordeaux is known in the English-speaking world, production of white wine is considerably greater than that of red.

With occasional breaks arising from differences between London and Paris, claret has been drunk in England since the Middle Ages, when Bordeaux and the surrounding countryside became an English possession, remaining so for 300 years. The finest clarets come from four principal areas: the Médoc, part of which is considered to be the very finest district, Graves, Pomerol and St Émilion. Each makes wines of differing styles. Within these main areas are communes or parishes with names as famous as those of the areas themselves – Pauillac, for instance, Margaux and St Julien.

The most celebrated of the white wines of Bordeaux are those from the Sauternes area, which produces lusciously sweet dessert wines. Good, dry white wines are also made, some of the best of them in the Graves area.

Clearly, not all or even a majority of the wines from such a large and diverse region can be of superlative quality. Clarets can range from simple, sound wines to the fine products of such important properties as Château Latour and Château Margaux. Among the more basic grades are plain Bordeaux Rouge and Bordeaux Blanc; Bordeaux Supérieur is only a slightly better grade.

Only a fraction of the region's wines can be classed as 'fine'.

In general, the better wines bear the name of the château or estate where they are made. The standard of less elevated wines, such as those carrying the name of a commune or larger area, is on average high, so that while the price of wines from the better-known châteaux tends to be steep, there is good value to be found among such district or commune wines.

Bordeaux Clairet *(France)* A delicate, fruity red wine of low acidity. To be entitled to the appellation, it must originate from the region of Bordeaux. Its fermentation period is short, it has the body of one of the fuller rosés of France, and it is for drinking young. Good, economical wine for warm-weather consumption.

Bordeaux Rosé *(France)* Pink wine, made in Bordeaux and variable in quality. Nothing of outstanding merit.

Bordeaux Rouge, Blanc *(France)* Red or white wine, marketed as *Appellation Bordeaux Contrôlée*. Such wines can come from any part of the Bordeaux region, though they are usually from peripheral districts which cannot claim a superior appellation. The reds should have some pretentions to the generally accepted style of claret, dry and with some measure of fruitiness. The whites may be dry or medium sweet. No wines sold under these plain appellations are ever great wines, though they are of respectable quality, especially the dry whites, and make agreeable drinking at a modest price.

Bordeaux Supérieur *(France)* Appellation for red or white wines produced within the Bordeaux region. To acquire the appellation, the wines must attain a prescribed level of alcohol. Many wines bearing this appellation are carefully blended to create something that has the general characteristics of claret or white Bordeaux. They are never outstanding wines, but many are of sound quality and make acceptable drinking at a reasonable price.

bottle age Some light wines, especially reds, can improve if allowed to age in bottle, while others will deteriorate. See **mature, maturity**.

bottle sickness An affliction that some wines may suffer as a consequence of the filtration process prior to bottling. Normally, the condition passes with time.

Bourg *(France)* A lesser district of Bordeaux, producing red and white wines. The area is often lumped together with the neighbouring district of Blaye, but its red wines have a discernibly fuller body and if allowed to develop in bottle they will acquire some of the distinction of better-rated Bordeaux reds. They may be sold as Bourgeais or Côtes de Bourg. Reds make a useful, economical substitute for pricier wines from elsewhere in Bordeaux; whites have no particular distinction.

bourgeois, cru bourgeois *(France)* An unofficial rating of vineyards in Bordeaux, based on usage of the various *crus*. Some of the properties listed produce wines of great distinction, though they are never fine wines. The *bourgeois* clarets of Bordeaux can represent exceptionally good value.

Bourgogne *(France)* The same as Burgundy.

Bourgogne Aligoté *(France)* White wine made in Burgundy solely or mainly from the Aligoté grape which yields an agreeable, light, short-lived wine of little distinction.

Bourgogne Blanc, Rouge *(France)* A lowly, though not the lowest, appellation for the plainer wines of Burgundy.

Bourgogne Grand Ordinaire *(France)* Appellation of the lowest order of Burgundy, despite the '*grand*' description. It is often of low strength.

Bourgueil *(France)* District of the Loire and producer of one of the better of France's lesser red wines, made from the Cabernet grape. It is fresh, moderately full-bodied, with a distinctive bouquet, and is at its best when consumed young.

Bouzy *(France)* Village in the Champagne region producing grapes for Champagne production and a still red wine, Bouzy Rouge. It is entitled to the appellation Coteaux de Champagne.

branded wines Proprietary wines, blended in a consistent style to the requirements of the brand owner. There are many long-established brand names, especially among sherries, but the number has rapidly increased during the past 20 years. This is due to the growth of the market in the UK for inexpensive light wines with easy-to-pronounce names and the abandonment of borrowing famous place names (such as Spanish 'Sauternes', for example) in an attempt to identify the general style of cheap wines.

Braunberg *(Germany)* District of the Mosel-Saar-

Ruwer area, and one of the most distinguished in this region. In a fine year Braunberg produces one of the best and most delicate wines to be found in Germany.

British wine A type of wine, usually fortified, made in the UK from imported grape juice. It comes in dry, medium and sweet styles; it is usually cheap but never good. Its sole attribute is that it is a wine of quite high alcoholic strength at a fairly modest price. It must not be confused with wine made in England from grapes grown in English vineyards. That is English, not British, wine.

Brouilly *(France)* A section of the red wine Beaujolais area and one of the most important. Its wines have the fresh fruitiness that is typical of the best Beaujolais growth and while it has some robustness, it is comparatively short-lived and needs to be consumed early.

Brown sherry *(Spain)* Richly sweet dessert wine, dark brown in colour and with a hint of caramel in the flavour.

Brunello *(Italy)* A variety of the Sangiovese grape. In Tuscany it makes a deep, long-lasting red wine, which is full tasting and dark in colour.

brut *(France)* Term applied to a very dry style of Champagne and other sparkling wines.

Bual, Boal *(Portugal)* A sweet style of Madeira. This dessert wine is comparable to a sweet sherry, though heavier.

Bulgaria One of the world's most prolific wine producers, using advanced methods. An extensive variety of wines is made from Western European and native grapes. Reds, which are generally heavy, full-bodied wines with sometimes more than a hint of sweetness in them, are made from the Cabernet, Kadarka, and Gamza grapes, among others. The whites, usually of a better standard than the reds, include good dry and medium-dry Rieslings, Chardonnays and Sylvaners. A version of the Muscat grape is used to produce an agreeable spicy, dry white wine, although many dessert wines based on the Muscat grape are also produced.

Bull's Blood *(Hungary)* This is a famous red wine produced in vineyards around the town of Eger in Hungary. It is deep in colour and in flavour, and has the distinction of being one of a few relatively inexpensive red wines that will show a marked improvement if left to mature in bottle for a few years.

Burgenland *(Austria)* A province with vineyards bordering Hungary, of which Burgenland was once a part. Some Hungarian influence remains in the viticulture especially in the cultivation of the Furmint grape, which makes good white dessert wines. Sound, dry whites are made from the Welsch-Riesling grape.

Burgundy *(France)* One of the world's most important fine wine regions, with reds and whites of great distinction, plus a good deal of ordinary wine. The characteristics of the wines vary from commune to commune and plot to plot, but the general expectation of a good red Burgundy is that it will be a rich, warm wine with a generous flavour. The Pinot Noir is the region's outstanding red wine grape. White Burgundy, made from the Chardonnay grape, is dry, attractively perfumed and full-flavoured. Sparkling wines – red, white and rosé – are also made, but only a few have any merit.

Placenames in Burgundy are somewhat complicated, in no small part due to the fact that a number of communes, or parishes, have annexed the name of their most cherished vineyards. Examples are Gevrey-Chambertin, where Gevrey is the parish name and Chambertin the name of the finest vineyard in it, and Nuits-St-Georges, a name the citizens of Nuits contrived by joining that of the good vineyard of Les St-Georges to the name of their town. Still more confusingly, Nuits is in a district called Côte de Nuits, which embraces a variety of vineyards producing wines some of which are finer than and some inferior to those of Nuits-St-Georges itself.

Another common feature in Burgundy is that many vineyards are divided into lots, each with its own proprietor, and there are varying degrees of proficiency and general approach among the proprietors. It is thus possible to find wines from the same vineyard and the same vintage which differ quite markedly in quality and character.

For these reasons, a knowledge of the names of the most reputable shippers in Burgundy is as important as a knowledge of the area and its wines. A shipper with a reputation to uphold will not sell an indifferent wine simply because it comes from a highly rated vineyard. The list of such shippers is a long one so these are only some of the best-known names:

Bouchard Aîné	J. Mommesin
J. Calvet & Cie.	Pasquier-Desvignes & Cie.

Joseph Drouhin	Piat Père & Fils
Georges Duboeuf	Jules Regnier & Cie.
J. Faiveley	J.B. Reynier
Geisweiler & Fils	Ropiteau Frères
Louis Jadot	L. Rosenheim & Sons Ltd
Louis Latour	Sichel & Cie.
de Marcilly Frères	Sichel & Fils Frères
Pierre Maufoux	Jean Thorin

The region is divided into five separate districts: Chablis, Côte d'Or, Chalonnais, Mâconnais and Beaujolais.

Byrrh *(France)* A branded wine-based aperitif flavoured with quinine.

Cabernet This is the forename of two grape varieties. The more distinguished is the Cabernet Sauvignon, used in the Médoc region of France to make, together with other grapes, the finest styles of claret.

It is also cultivated widely in other wine-producing countries, for example in Australia, Chile and the United States, producing wines of a similar style to claret, though never with the same distinction as the better clarets.

Cabernet Franc is a more prolific and therefore less distinguished grape variety grown in other districts of Bordeaux, notably in St-Émilion. It is also the grape that gives its name to the better-rated rosé wines of the Loire valley.

Cadaujac *(France)* An important commune of the Graves area. Red and white wines of good quality are produced here. Château Bouscaut is one of the principal properties.

Cadillac *(France)* White wine commune of the Premières Côtes de Bordeaux making sound, sweet and semi-sweet wines.

Cahors *(France)* A district in central France making lusty red wine once known as 'the black wine of Cahors' because of the depth of its colour, and at one time a rival of claret. In recent years a good deal of it has become much less dark, owing to changing methods of vinification. However, wines made by the ancient method are still to be found, and are very rewarding, taking many years to reach maturity. Some versions of Cahors on the UK market are disappointingly light compared to the weightiness this wine ought to have, but prices are usually moderate, so that they are one of the good, quite deeply flavoured wines within the reach of most purses.

California *(USA)* This is the great vineyard area

of North America, producing a variety of styles, mostly light wines. Much indifferent wine is made but the better products are of markedly high quality. Californian methods of cultivation and production are among the most progressive in the world. European vines are used and quality wines are generally marketed under the variety they are made from. The Chardonnay, Riesling (known in California as Johannisberger Riesling), Sauvignon Blanc and Chenin grapes make some of the top-grade whites, while reds in this category are made from the Cabernet Sauvignon, Pinot Noir, Merlot and the Gamay (known as the Gamay Beaujolais). The Grenache makes some good rosés. A grape variety of unknown origin, but almost certainly a transplant from Europe and the most widely cultivated vine in California, is the Zinfandel, producing a lightish red.

The Napa Valley is the best area; others of note include Sonoma, Livermore, Santa Clara, San Benito and Monterey. A good representative selection of Californian wines is available in the UK. Dependable producers' names include the Christian Brothers (a monastic teaching order), Mondavi, Joseph Phelps, Paul Masson and Louis Martini. California is also a producer of fortified wines but in general they are not of outstanding quality and are not readily available in the UK.

Campania *(Italy)* A major wine region, producer of Lacrima Christi and the wines of the islands of Capri and Ischia.

Canonau *(Italy)* A stout red wine from the island of Sardinia suitable for everyday drinking.

Canon-Fronsac *(France)* A small red wine zone within the district of Fronsac. It is entitled to its own appellation and makes big, robust wines that are generally superior in quality to those of Fronsac.

Cantenac *(France)* Commune in the Haut-Médoc making good-quality claret and possessing a number of notable vineyards, including Château Brane-Cantenac, a second growth, and Château Palmer, Kirwan, Boyd-Cantenac, d'Issan and Cantenac-Brown, all third growths. The wines are of the general character of those of the Margaux district.

Cap Corse *(Corsica)* A fortified aperitif from Corsica with a flavour strident enough to take the drinker's breath away. Heavy and earthy, it is good stuff for bandits.

Cape wines see **South Africa**

carafe A glass container for wine. In France *Vin de carafe* is young, inexpensive wine.

carbonated wine A wine rendered fizzy by the introduction of carbon dioxide. It is a short, inexpensive route to making 'sparkling' wine, but the sparkle does not last for long and no wines of any merit are treated in this way. Carbonated wine will be the least attractive of any sparkling wine.

Carema *(Italy)* Red wine made from the Nebbiolo grape. Generally softer and easier to drink than other Italian wines produced from this variety, and therefore less stately. Carema comes from an area near Turin.

Cassis *(France)* A good district of the Provence region producing well-flavoured, strong white and rosé wines. There is nothing especially outstanding in their quality but they have the distinctive assertiveness that characterizes many of the wines of Provence. Some red is also made, but it is of little consequence.

Catalonia *(Spain)* Large region in the north east, where an extensive variety of wines is made – red, white, rosé, sparkling and fortified. The bulk of it is of fairly ordinary quality and is used for blending into inexpensive brands. Important districts include Alella, Panadés and Tarragona.

cépage *(France)* Term referring to the variety of grape vine used, such as the Pinot Noir, Chardonnay and Muscat.

Cérons *(France)* Village near the communes of Sauternes and Barsac making sweet and semi-sweet white wines. The appellation Cérons also embraces the communes of Illats and Podensac. In a good year, when the grapes have an opportunity to reach an advanced state of ripeness, the sweet wines are close to the style of Barsac. Some dry wines are also made in the district.

Chablis *(France)* A renowned white wine district of Burgundy. The wine is all dry and the finest, classed as Chablis Grand Cru, has a distinctive, steely dryness with a clean fresh finish. The next best category, Chablis Premier Cru, will have a good showing of these attributes. A third appellation is simply Chablis, and should be expected to offer no more than the general character of the wine of the district in a shallower way than the two higher categories. Petit Chablis, a light, quaffing wine, is the lowest category. All Chablis is for drinking while it is still young and fresh. Vintages are of special importance, for a poor one can produce wines so sharp and thin as to be disagreeable.

Vineyard names of note include Vaudésir, Les Clos, Grenouilles, Valmur, Blanchots, Les Preuses and Bourgros – the seven sites entitled to the *grand cru* appellation.

Chalonnais *(France)* Secondary area of Burgundy, lying to the south of the Côte de Beaune and producing some red and white wines of good quality, but without the finesse and depth of the best Burgundian wines. The Pinot Noir is the important grape for red wines, the Chardonnay and Pinot Blanc for whites. Generally the reds are fairly light for Burgundies but are often attractively perfumed, and of a better standard than the whites. The area also produces considerable quantities of sparkling wine, which is of little interest. The best-known communes are Mercurey, Montagny, Givry and Rully.

Chambéry *(France)* A district in the Savoie region noted for its delicate, lightly flavoured, dry vermouth. There is a strawberry version.

Chambolle-Musigny *(France)* One of the great

communes of the Côte de Nuits, producing red and a small quantity of white wines. The reds are rated as some of the most stylish and fragrant of all Burgundies and come from such notable vineyards as Les Musigny, Les Amoureuses, and the major section of Les Bonnes Mares which lies within the commune's boundaries. Les Musigny also produces some fine dry white wine, Musigny Blanc.

Champagne *(France)* A famous region in northwest France, producing what is indisputably the greatest of the world's sparkling wines. Others try to make similar wines elsewhere, using the *méthode champenoise* and the traditional grapes of Champagne, the Pinot Noir, Pinot Meunier and the Chardonnay. But, though capable of producing sparkling wines that are good and sometimes distinguished, the emulators never succeed in wholly capturing the elegant style of Champagne itself. In the UK, and in most Western countries, the name Champagne is lawfully applied only to the wines from the Champagne area of France, but elsewhere in the world the name is freely borrowed for any sparkling wine.

Although most of the wines are made from a mixture of red and white grapes, the skins of the black grapes are separated from the juice before they can impart their colour to it. Thus the great majority of Champagne is white; however, some rosé or pink Champagne is also produced. The wine can vary from very dry to very sweet, depending on the quantity of sugar solution added during production. The driest styles are labelled *dry*, *extra dry*, *extra sec*, or *brut*. Rather less dry styles are labelled *sec* or *demi-sec* and the sweetest style of all is *rich*. In Champagne descriptions, the word 'sec', although it means dry, does not indicate a specially dry style.

There are four production centres: Ay, Épernay, Reims and Tours-sur-Marne. Reims has the largest number of Champagne houses with names that are familiar on the British market – Charles Heidsieck, Lanson, Krug, Pommery-Greno, Roederer, Taittinger and Veuve-Clicquot are among them. Almost all Champagne is sold under such house names, but some British merchants have established their own brand names, buying direct from one or other of the Champagne producers. Often such wines come from distinguished producers and, being sold at prices usually below those of the best-known names, can offer remarkably good value for money.

Most Champagne is a blend of wine from different vintages but in exceptionally good years a producer may declare a vintage, and will sell that wine as a vintage wine. Several Champagne producers also have a 'de luxe' version of their brand. Both vintage Champagne and the de luxe versions command a premium price.

Chardonnay An outstanding white grape variety and primary constituent of the finest styles of white Burgundy. It is also an important constituent of Champagne.

Chassagne-Montrachet *(France)* Commune of the Côte de Beaune, celebrated for its dry white wines. Its finest vineyard, Le Montrachet, lies partly in the neighbouring commune of Puligny-Montrachet, as does another notable vineyard, Bâtard-Montrachet. Le Montrachet makes a fine mellow, full wine, very much in demand and very expensive. Bâtard-Montrachet is just about as distinguished, and shared with the commune of Puligny-Montrachet, other fine vineyards include Criots-Bâtard-Montrachet and Les Ruchottes. Less stately wines, simply labelled Chassagne-Montrachet, can be extremely good. Some red is made but it is of small importance.

Chasselas The leading grape variety of Switzerland, where it is called the Fendant. It is also grown in Germany and known there as the

Gutedel. In these northerly areas, and with the right conditions, it can produce a respectable but light wine, usually short-lived. The grape is also grown in Alsace (France), where it provides a base for blended wines.

Château *(France)* In wine terminology this can refer to a farmhouse, country house or castle with its own vineyards. The word *château* on a label does not necessarily imply that the wine is of outstanding merit. There are several hundred properties in France describing themselves as *châteaux*, but only a minority of wines so labelled come into the category of fine wine.

Château bottled A Bordeaux wine that has been bottled on the estate where it has been produced. The term indicates a guarantee that the wine is authentic, though recent regulations, emanating mainly from the EEC, have made the need for this form of guarantee less important.

Château-Chalon *(France)* Not a castle or estate, but a hamlet in the Jura area making an original white wine similar in flavour to a dry sherry. Unlike sherry, however, the wine is not fortified with spirit, but it is matured in cask for six years in a process not unlike that used in sherry production. Wines from Château-Chalon are good but expensive, and those looking for a wine of this style would pay less for a good dry sherry.

Châteauneuf-du-Pape *(France)* District of the Rhône region famous for its red wines but also producing some whites. The reds are strong, sun-warmed wines that can attain great smoothness with age. Up to 13 grape varieties may be used, so that the *vigneron* has considerable latitude to produce his own style of Châteauneuf-du-Pape and the wines therefore show appreciable differences between one producer and another. Red Châteauneuf-du-Pape becomes round and mellow after only about three or four years in bottle. The whites can be agreeable but have little distinction.

Chénas *(France)* One of the nine important communes of Beaujolais producing good, fresh, light red wines typical of the general Beaujolais style, though seldom attaining the heights of the very best of the nine communes.

Chenin Blanc A variety of white grape prominent in the Loire Valley of France and the primary grape for such wines as Vouvray and Saumur. The Chenin Blanc is also cultivated elsewhere, notably in California.

Chianti *(Italy)* Good red wine from Tuscany. Most of it is light, fresh wine intended to be consumed immediately. Chianti Riserva is a wine with five years or more cask age, and with bottle age will continue to improve, acquiring great body and finesse. Chianti Classico is a wine from a delimited district lying between Florence and Siena, and is generally rated more highly than wines from other districts in the Chianti area. White Chianti was made obsolete under Italian wine laws introduced in 1963. The wine that was formerly sold under the name is now likely to be sold as Vino Bianco Toscana.

Chiaretto del Garda *(Italy)* A good, light, pale fresh rosé from the shores of Lake Garda. Considered to be one of the best rosé wines made in Italy, it is quite low in alcohol and must be consumed early while it retains its freshness.

Chile This is the oldest wine-producing country in South America, with an industry established for over 350 years. French cuttings and French experts brought to the country in the mid-nineteenth century created a sound basis for the modern industry. The Chilean wine most often encountered in the UK is a good quality red made from the Cabernet grape and is usually cheaper than wines of comparable quality from Europe.

Chinon *(France)* Good, fresh, fairly full-bodied red wine which takes its name from the village of Chinon in the Loire region. Made from the Cabernet grape, this is a wine to drink when it is young.

Chiroubles *(France)* A commune of the Beaujolais area and ranking among the best of the celebrated red wine communes of that district. It possesses the typical fruitiness of a good-class Beaujolais, is light in body and quick to mature. Unlikely to gain anything by being kept in bottle, it should be consumed as soon as it is available after the vintage.

Cinsault A grape variety used in making red wine, especially as a component of blends. Some of these are highly rated – Châteauneuf-du-Pape, for instance.

Clairette de Die *(France)* An unsubtle, usually rather sweet, white sparkling wine from Die in the Rhône region. It has a noticeable Muscat flavour.

Clairette du Languedoc *(France)* One of the

few passable dry white wines produced in the Languedoc-Roussillon area. Another wine of similar style is Clairette de Bellegarde. Though notable among the fairly common white wines of the area, they are of no special merit.

claret Traditional name in England for the red wines of Bordeaux. The name has no legal definition, but in the UK it should mean red Bordeaux. In the United States it can mean any red light wine.

Classico *(Italy)* The centre of the Chianti district in Tuscany.

classifications A French notion, begun well over a century ago and never completed. The original and most notable classification was set out in 1855, specifically for the World Exhibition which took place in Paris that year, when the red wines of the Médoc were placed in five classes. The classification was prepared by a committee of wine experts and brokers, whose judgment was influenced not only by the quality of the wines but by the prices they were then fetching. At the same time, the committee classified the vineyards of Sauternes. Despite the somewhat subjective criteria by which the committee had reached its

conclusions, and the various changes in the own-
ership of vineyards that have since taken place,
this nineteenth-century assessment remains largely accurate. (See page 64.)

The original 1855 classification included one red
wine growth that does happen to be outside the
Médoc; this was Château Haut-Brion, a notable
vineyard in Graves. In 1973, the wine of Château
Mouton-Rothschild was, by government decree,
elevated from 'second growth' rank to 'first
growth'. This, so far, is the only change in the
original classification of the Médoc wines, but in
1953 an official classification of the wines of
Graves was promulgated, and in 1955 an official
classification was made of the 'great growths' of
St-Émilion. There has never been an official
classification of the wines of Pomerol although, in
practice, its best wines are widely known.

Clastidio *(Italy)* Red, white and rosé wines from
Lombardy. The white Clastidio is the only wine
of distinction, made from a mix of local grapes. It
is a light dessert wine, golden in colour.

clos *(France)* A vineyard or group of vineyards
which is, or has been, enclosed by a wall. It is a
fairly common prefix to vineyard names in Burgundy, but also occurs elsewhere in France.

Commandaria *(Cyprus)* Historically, the great wine of Cyprus, but changing tastes have largely left behind big, strong, very sweet wines of this kind. It is a rich, dark-coloured wine, made from red and white grapes that are allowed to lie out in the sun until they are dry so that they have a high concentration of sugar. The original Commandaria was painstakingly made and left to mature for many years. Possibly some of it receives the same treatment today, but much Commandaria is now made on a commercial basis and lacks the appeal that originally gave it world fame. On the UK market, an unaged Commandaria will be no more than a rather unsatisfactory dessert wine, too heavy and too solid, with nothing of the grandeur of the old-style wine.

commune *(France)* A parish, a village or a cluster of villages forming a wine-producing district.

Condrieu *(France)* A small district of the Rhône region making good dry and semi-dry white wines, golden in colour, fruity and sometimes *pétillant*. They are unlikely to improve with bottle age, and are best consumed when young. In this district is the famous vineyard of Château Grillet, the smallest to possess its own appellation, producing prized white wines that are dry with a full flavour. But production is small and prices are very high.

Consorzio *(Italy)* A local association or guild of wine producers, usually setting standards of quality before permitting its members to use the mark of the Consorzio on their bottles. Before the introduction of State controls, the Consorzi were responsible for quality and authenticity. The best-known mark or crest is that of the Consorzio of Chianti Classico – a black rooster.

Corbières *(France)* A good district of the Languedoc-Roussillon area making red, white and rosé wines, of which the amply-flavoured reds are the best.

corkage This is the charge levied by some restaurants and hotels if they discover you have brought wines or spirits on to their premises and consumed them there. Unlicensed restaurants do not, generally, impose such a charge since they have no alternative to offer.

Cornas *(France)* Red wine district of the Rhône region. Few of the wines are rated highly. Young wines can be harsh, but in general they can be expected to become more benign with bottle age.

Corriente, Vino *(Spain)* Any wine in a restaurant or bar that is immediately available; the current wine, the wine of the house, or the wine on tap.

Corsica *(France)* Mediterranean island, a *département* of France. Viticulture has steadily advanced in standard since the resettlement in Corsica of wine growers who came to the island from Algeria, and the island now has several vineyards making *appellation contrôlée* wines. Patrimonio is one, most notable for rosé wines made from the Grenache grape but also producing acceptable reds and whites; another is Coteaux d'Ajaccio, the slopes lying around the capital of the island and producing good reds and rosés. Sartène is an area known for its lusty reds.

The wines of Corsica have, in general, little refinement. They are strong, bulky and husky but they are, for the most part, good honest wines. If comparison is possible with wines from any part of the mainland, the best can be compared with some of those from the Languedoc-Roussillon area in southern France.

Cortaillod see **Neuchâtel**

Corton see **Aloxe-Corton**

Corvo di Salaparuta *(Italy)* Dry red or white wines from Sicily, well above average among the wines of the island. The red is outstanding, low in acidity and with a good velvety texture.

Costières-du-Gard *(France)* Red, white and rosé wine-producing district in the area of Languedoc-Roussillon. The better wines are the reds which, although light, are well made and inexpensive.

Côte *(France)* A slope planted with vines. On labels, the word appears as a prefix to an area or district name, for example, Côte de Beaune. Wines so labelled will be of lesser merit than a wine from the same area that is entitled to use a specific commune name.

Côte de Beaune *(France)* Fine wine district in the south of the Côte d'Or making some of the best red and white wines in Burgundy, but especially acclaimed for whites, which are dry, firm and full-flavoured and sometimes benefit by spending three or more years in bottle. The reds tend to be softer, more supple and quicker to mature than those from the more northerly part of the Côte d'Or, although there are some important exceptions. These are wines which are sold under a commune name such as Pommard or Volnay and a number of villages may label their wine Côte de Beaune Villages. The finest communes are Aloxe-Corton, Savigny-les-Beaune, Beaune, Pommard, Volnay, Chassagne-Montrachet, Meursault and Puligny-Montrachet.

Côte de Nuits *(France)* Most northerly part of the famous Côte d'Or district in Burgundy, overflowing with renowned red wine names. There are considerable variations in the style of wines made here, but in general they are generously flavoured, firm, full-bodied and long lasting. Plainer wines may be named after the commune in which they are made. Côte de Nuits Villages is the appellation for the wines of certain specified villages, likely to be blended and on much the same level as the commune wines, while the most outstanding individual vineyards may use their own name, often, but not always, accompanied by the commune name.

Notable red wine commune names are Fixin, Gevrey-Chambertin, Morey-St-Denis, Chambolle-Musigny, Vougeot, Flagey-Échezeaux, Vosne-Romanée and Nuits-St-Georges. Vougeot and Chambolle-Musigny also make good white wines.

Côte d'Or *(France)* The famous 'golden slope' of

Burgundy, full of famous communes and vine-yards making distinguished red and white wines. The name is not an official appellation and no producer may sell his wine as such. The district is divided into two important sections, the Côte de Nuits and the Côte de Beaune.

Côte Rôtie *(France)* The 'roasted slope', rated among the best districts in the Rhône region. The wines are full-bodied reds and have an intense bouquet. They are long-lived and will improve markedly with age, becoming sleek and velvety.

Coteaux Champenois *(France)* Still, light wine made in the Champagne region, otherwise known as Vin Natur de la Champagne. It may be white or red. Both are slenderly flavoured with little outstanding merit, though they are generally highly priced.

Coteaux de la Loire *(France)* A district of Anjou making mainly sweet or semi-sweet white wines. Some are made by the method used in the production of Sauternes, in which grapes are left ungathered until they have a considerable con-centration of sugar. The district also produces Muscadet, usually without the delicacy of others from the Loire.

Coteaux du Layon *(France)* A district of the Loire producing a variety of styles and qualities, but notable for fragrant, rich, sweet whites of great smoothness, the finest of which are comparable with good Sauternes. The best-known site is Quarts de Chaume.

Côtes de Brouilly *(France)* An outstanding red wine commune of the Beaujolais area. The wine of this parish tends to have more fullness than some of the other famous growths of the region, but it has the characteristic Beaujolais fruitiness and a fine bouquet. It is a wine for drinking a year of two after the vintage of its birth.

Côtes de Castillon *(France)* District of Bordeaux near St-Émilion making wines of a similar style. Not outstanding, but relatively low prices make for relaxed drinking. The district has its own appellation.

Côtes du Rhône *(France)* Appellation for the lesser wines, red, white and rosé, of the Rhône valley. Red wine sold under the appellation can often be of sound quality, sometimes approaching the standards of higher appellations in the region.

cradle A cradle-shaped wine basket designed to

hold a bottle in a horizontal position so that, on being withdrawn from the wine bin, the sediment is not disturbed. Now largely redundant, since wines do not carry the quantity of sediment they once did, the cradle is still used as a picturesque frill in some restaurants. Any wine that requires a cradle should more properly have been withdrawn from the bin many hours before it is to be consumed to allow the sediment to settle. After this, it can be decanted off the sediment.

Cream sherry *(Spain)* A full, lusciously sweet dessert wine usually dark in colour, although in recent years Pale Cream sherries have been introduced to the British market.

crémant *(France)* The term for a creamy, moderately sparkling wine; it does not have the full sparkle of typical Champagnes.

Crépy *(France)* A good light, dry white wine produced in Savoie. Some of it is naturally semi-sparkling.

Crozes-Hermitage *(France)* Red and white wines of the Rhône region. Grown on the hill of Hermitage but in vineyards lower down the hillside, the wines are less distinguished than those entitled to the Hermitage appellation. Most of the production is red, but the whites are often of excellent quality. Crozes-Hermitage makes an acceptable and economical alternative to Hermitage.

cru *(France)* A term meaning vineyard, or growth. In France the word has a special distinction because some of the most important wines have been classified into grades of growth – first growth, second growth, and so on. The appearance of the word *cru* on a label suggests a wine that is in some way superior to others within its district or region of origin.

crust The hardened sediment which forms in bottles of older port. The wine needs to be decanted off the crust.

Crusted port Good quality port, not necessarily of a single vintage, bottled early for laying down to improve in bottle. The crust is the sediment that forms inside the bottle, and Crusted port, like Vintage port, needs to be decanted. It has been superseded to a great extent by Late-bottled Vintage port.

cuve close A method of producing sparkling

wines on a large scale. The wine is passed through a series of closed tanks, where it is artificially aged by changes of temperature, fermented, and clarified. The *cuve close* process is used for inexpensive wines but the result never bears comparison with wines made by the *méthode champenoise*. Generally the flavour is shorter and the bubbles soon diminish.

cuvée *(France)* Literally, this term means the contents of a vat and usually refers to wine that has been made in the same *cuve* (vat or cask), or has the same origin. On a wine label or list, the word has assumed a dignified meaning in the UK. *Première cuvée* suggests a wine of major importance; so does *tête de cuvée*. But while these terms are intended to indicate a wine of above-average quality, this cannot always be assured.

Cyprus An important Mediterranean island, best known on the UK market as a producer of sherry-style wines at a competitive price (see **Cyprus sherry**). It is also a significant source of inexpensive light wines, red, white and rosé. Several of these offer good value, notably the reds; their fullness manages to contain to some extent the warm, almost burnt, flavour that typifies light wines from a warm climate. In recent years

Cyprus has thoroughly modernized her wine industry, investing £10 million on new plant and equipment, with the result that this former British territory is now one of the most technically advanced wine producers in the world. The economy of Cyprus depends heavily on wine production and the country is attempting to break away from its image as a producer of cheaply priced and indifferent wines.

Apart from modernization, one result of this has been the introduction, on an experimental basis, of a considerable quantity of traditional European vine plants. Those that have so far shown signs of promise include Cabernet Sauvignon, Riesling, Sauvignon Blanc, Chardonnay, and Sémillon. Research is continuing.

The light wines of Cyprus are marketed under brand names. Examples are Othello and Kolossi, both full-bodied reds; Aphrodite, a middle-of-the-road white; the white version of Kolossi, which is reasonably dry; Bellapais, an uncommon white wine for a warm area in that it is light in flavour and is slightly *pétillant*; and Rosella, a pink wine which is drinkable enough but with too much sweetness to rank as a serious rosé. The historically famous wine of Cyprus is Commandaria, big and sweet and a dessert wine of considerable reputation.

Cyprus sherry A variable sherry-style wine from Cyprus. The best can have some of the essential flavours of real sherry, which comes only from the Spanish district of Jerez, but most of it does not display convincing sherry characteristics, especially the drier styles, which often have a flavour more akin to vermouth than to sherry. Yet such wines have an entrenched position on the UK market, mainly on account of their cheapness. In general, the medium-sweet and sweet versions offer better value for money than do the dry varieties.

Dão *(Portugal)* Mountain district south of the port-wine making region. It is notable for its deep-coloured red wines, which have considerable body and a fine fruity flavour. They can become very stylish if given a few years in bottle. The main grape varieties are those used in the production of port. White wines form only a small proportion of the total production. They are of no special distinction, for early consumption.

Deidesheim *(Germany)* Town in the Rheinpfalz region with a number of surrounding vineyards which make some of the finest wines of the region. Most are made from the noble Riesling grape. There are several especially notable vine-

yards including the romantically named Paradies-
garten as well as Hohenmorgen, Langenmorgen
and Nonnenstück.

De Luxe Champagne *(French)* Superior and
costly wines made from high-quality grapes by a
number of the leading Champagne houses. Examples include Moët and Chandon's Dom Pérignon,
Roederer's Cristal and Heidsieck's Diamant Bleu.

demi-sec *(France)* Literally, this means 'half dry'.
On a Champagne label, however, the words
indicate one of the sweeter styles. A dry Champagne will be labelled *dry*, *extra dry*, *extra sec* or
brut, and this usage is common among other
producers of French sparkling wines.

**Denominazione di Origine Controllata
(DOC)** *(Italy)* In 1963 a presidential decree in
Rome introduced a law controlling the denomina-
tion of origin of Italian wines. It meant that a
producer cannot make or sell a wine under a name
that implies that it comes from a particular area
unless it has been produced in that area, from
certified vineyards, with certified varieties of
grapes in the right proportions and made, aged
and bottled according to specifications laid down.
 Long before the new law of 1963 many well

known and highly prized wines were controlled by the Consorzio in order to protect typical wines. The Chianti Consorzio obtained the force of law for the territorial limits for Classico Chianti production as early as 1932. The official limits for Marsala production go back to 1931, and were redefined in 1951. Under the ultimate authority of Italy's Ministry of Agriculture, control is in the hands of a body composed of grape growers, wine producers, dealers, members of professional associations, state experts, and the National Union of Consumers, plus five civil servants.

This means that the DOC label on a bottle should ensure that the wine is from the area named; that it is produced from the different grapes in the proportions laid down, and by the traditional methods; that the vineyards have been surveyed and their maximum grape production not exceeded; and that the yield of wine per ton of grapes is within the permitted limits. It should also guarantee that the wine has been inspected during maturation and storage by official inspectors; all sales of the wine from producer to wholesaler and bottler have been recorded carefully in ledgers subject to inspection; the vintage date is correct; misleading labels are not used; and further, when all these other conditions are satisfied, that the wine itself has met high standards of taste, flavour, bouquet, chemical, alcohol and acid content. The DOC is hard to win.

The law allows not only the producers to apply for the DOC but also the Consorzio, other wine growers' organizations and bodies such as Chambers of Commerce. The controlling committee can step in to seek recognition if none of these apply. Apart from the inspectorate of the Ministry of Agriculture, the supervision under the DOC law can be given to voluntary Consorzi. They can undertake prosecutions and their staff may act as part of the judicial police force.

Regulations on labelling are strict and, among other things, labels that mystify the consumer are not allowed. No words like 'type' are permitted.

Plain misuse of the DOC title or forging a label carries a heavy fine and imprisonment. In particularly grave cases, the offending producer or merchant can have his products confiscated and his establishment closed for up to a year.

dessert wine A wine of distinct sweetness, traditionally served with the dessert course. Examples are Sauternes, rich Champagne, Tokay, the very sweet styles of German wines like Trockenbeerenauslese, port, Cream sherry and the richer styles of Madeira, especially Malmsey, Malaga and Marsala.

Deutscher Tafelwein *(Germany)* The term for plain table wine. To use the word on a label the producer must ensure the wine conforms to specific requirements under German wine law. It has to come from designated areas and be made from stated grape varieties grown only in Germany. It is at the lower end of the quality scale for German wines. Quality and character are variable, but in general it is a light, fresh, quaffing wine, often sold in litres, for early consumption.

Deutsches Weinsiegel *(Germany)* A seal, sometimes encountered on German wine bottles, denoting that the wine has been judged to be of especially high quality. The wines are assessed by the Deutsche Landwirtschafts-Gesellschaft, the German Agricultural Society, which is an independent body.

Dézaley *(Switzerland)* Dry white wine of the canton of Vaud made from the Chasselas (Fendant) grape.

Dienheim *(Germany)* Town and wine-producing district of the Rheinhessen region. The wines are soft and round, and in a good year they have considerable elegance, but Dienheim is not one of the greatest districts of the region. A notable producer here is Staatsweingut, the State wine domain.

DOC *(Italy)* *Denominazione di Origine Controllata.* Shorthand for a wine with a pedigree; the Italian equivalent of the French *appellation contrôlée*. See **Denominazione di Origine Controllata**.

DOCG *(Italy)* *Denominazione di Origine Controllata e Garantita.* A superior guarantee under Italian wine law, reserved for only the most outstanding of the DOC wines. See **Denominazione di Origine Controllata**.

Dôle *(Switzerland)* A fairly full, soft, dark-coloured red made in the canton of Valais from Gamay and Pinot Noir grape varieties.

Domaine *(France)* The word means a vineyard or a parcel of vineyards. In Burgundy, they are not always adjacent, and the generalized names of a *domaine* may well spread over many miles, some separated by others. In Bordeaux it is customary to produce wine under the name of a single château, but *domaines* also figure here, although they will not be as dispersed as they are in Burgundy. A Bordeaux *domaine* will be a single, uninterrupted area of land.

Dorin *(Switzerland)* Generic name for white wines produced in Vaud.

DOS *(Italy) Denominazione di Origine Semplice.* A plain guarantee of origin under Italian wine law. See **Denominazione di Origine Controllata**.

Doux Naturel, Vin *(France)* Sweet dessert wines, mainly from southern France. Despite the word '*naturel*', some are fortified with spirit.

dry Truly dry wine is one in which all the natural sugar in the grape juice is converted into alcohol during the fermentation process. Others can have some residual sugar, but not sufficient for them to taste sweet or semi-dry. Many wines described as dry, however, are dry only by contrast with the sweeter versions of wine in the same category. Notable among these are sherry brands which incorporate the word 'dry' in the brand name. There is no intention to deceive: the word is merely used to indicate that the wine is not sweet.

Dubonnet *(France)* A proprietary brand of aperitif based on wine and flavoured with quinine.

Dürkheim *(Germany)* Centre of a prolific wine-producing district in the Rheinpfalz region. The majority of the wines made here have no special distinction, but include some fine wines pressed from the Riesling grape. Spielberg and Ritterberg are among the best-known vineyards.

Edelfäule see **noble rot**

Edelzwicker *(France)* A blend of white wines produced in Alsace. *Edel* means noble, and the blend must be made from the 'noble' grapes of the region, such as Riesling, Sylvaner and Gewürztraminer. Such blends are well made and offer good value among Alsatian wines. See also **Zwicker**.

EEC Wine A blend of wines from countries in the European Economic Community. A popular version is made from German and Luxembourg wines.

Eger *(Hungary)* A town and wine-producing district notable for producing Bull's Blood and also some sound red and white wines.

Egri Bikavér see **Bulls' Blood**

Eiswein *(Germany)* Literally, the word means 'ice wine' and is the ultimate in the rare, sweet white wine category of Germany. Eiswein is made from grapes that have been left so late on the vine that they have become shrivelled and frozen. It is not uncommon for Eiswein grapes to remain in the vineyards until November or December and they are then pressed in their frozen state. The resultant wine is lusciously sweet, since it is highly concentrated in sugar and the essence of fruit. Eiswein is rarely made and when the right conditions occur, it is produced only in small quantities. It follows that it is extremely expensive.

éleveur *(France)* A middleman who buys a grower's product and looks after it while it matures. Then, in association with the *négociant*, he bottles and ships the wine. Frequently, the *éleveur* and the *négociant* are one and the same person.

Eltville *(Germany)* An important wine village of the Rheingau region. The vineyards make wines that are emphatically of the Rheingau style, with a considerable weight for a white wine. Taubenberg, Sonnenberg and Langenstück are among vineyards of note.

Emilia-Romagna *(Italy)* Large region producing few notable wines, with the exception of Lambrusco and some good reds made from the Sangiovese grape.

England The term 'English wine' embraces light wines made from grapes grown in England and Wales. English wine has experienced a revival in the past 20 years or so, after a long period in which vineyards were unproductive since the days of Henry VIII when vines were uprooted during the dissolution of the monasteries. Home-produced wine has caught the imagination of growers but not, so far, of the public, since its price and quality can almost always be bettered by imported wines.

The great majority of modern English vineyards lie in the South East, especially in Kent, Surrey, Sussex, Essex and Hampshire, but they extend north into Lincolnshire, south into Cornwall and Devon and across the country into Wales. English wines are generally dry, rather acidic and somewhat thin, except in very hot years such as 1976 when they can bear comparison with lesser wines from the Moselle.

Almost all the production is white, though some reds are made. The main grape varieties correspond to a great extent with those cultivated in Germany, another of Europe's northerly wine fields, Müller-Thurgau, Seyve-Villard, Pinot-Chardonnay, and Scheurebe among others. Regional and district names have little significance in England, but notable vineyard names include Hambledon (Hampshire), Felstar (Essex), Chilsdown (Sussex), Langham (Essex), Anderida (Isle of Wight), Biddenden (Kent), Pilton Manor (Somerset), Lamberhurst Priory (Kent), Adgestone (Isle of Wight) and Kelsall (Suffolk). English wines are not always easily available.

Entre-Deux-Mers *(France)* Large district of Bordeaux, devoted mainly to white wines of variable quality. Some red wine is made but it is not entitled to the appellation. The whites are of middle quality, mostly dry, made from the Sauvignon grape. Once rather low-grade, sweetish wines, there have been considerable and generally successful efforts to improve their standard in recent years. There are no outstanding vineyards.

Épernay *(France)* Town on the Marne River, notable as a centre of the Champagne industry. Firms based in Épernay include Mercier, Moët and Chandon and Pol Roger.

Erbach *(Germany)* Small but world-famous wine village of the Rheingau region. The fine vineyard of Markobrunn lies on the boundary between Erbach and the neighbouring village of Hattenheim, and traditionally the wine was sold simply as Marcobrunn. Now, under German wine law, it is sold as Erbacher Markobrunn. It has a profound flavour and bouquet and is one of Germany's best. There are, however, other good vineyards in Erbach making wine of a comparable style.

Escherndorf *(Germany)* Town in Franconia with vineyards that are among the most highly rated of that region. Among notable vineyards are Lump and Fürstenberg.

Espumoso *(Spain)* Sparkling wine which can attain high standards, especially in the small district of Perelada, near the Costa Brava. But in Spain some sparkling wine is labelled or sold as Champagne (or Xampan). This is correct only if the wine has come from the delimited Champagne region of France. It is not permitted in EEC countries and even in Spain it is a misnomer.

Essencia, Eszencia *(Hungary)* A very fine and luscious pressing of Tokay. The grapes are not pressed by machine or manually; the sheer weight of the over-ripe fruit causes the golden juice to run out, making the best-rated and most highly priced of all the wines of Tokay. It has always been a rarity.

estate bottled This refers to a wine that has been bottled by the producer, and a label containing this description is a form of guarantee that the wine is the authentic product of the vineyard named and that it has not been blended with an inferior wine. The practice tends to make wine more expensive, since small-scale bottling operations are not economical, while the cost of exporting wine in bottles is considerably greater than bulk shipments. Nevertheless, the practice has helped to reduce the 'faking' of wines.

Est! Est!! Est!!! *(Italy)* A sweet wine from Montefiascone in the Lazio region. It has no particular distinction apart from its name.

Ezerjó A white wine grape of Hungary, giving its name to a golden-coloured wine produced in the district of Mór, near Budapest.

Fargues *(France)* One of the five communes producing the famous sweet white wine of Sauternes to which appellation Fargues is entitled. The best-known vineyard is Château Rieussec.

Faugères *(France)* District of the Languedoc-Roussillon area making acceptable red wines of a fairly lightweight kind.

Fendant *(Switzerland)* The Swiss name for the white grape Chasselas, a high-yielding variety. It is also the name of the wine made from this grape in Valais.

fiasco *(Italy)* A straw-covered flask most commonly identified with Chianti, but it is not exclusive to the area and many lesser wines are bottled in such containers.

fine wine A term that has no precise definition, but which is generally applied to the best growths of France and Germany. A few other wines might also qualify, for instance Vintage port and the best styles of Tokay. Wines described as 'great' are fine wines from an especially good vintage.

Fino *(Spain)* One of the driest styles of sherry; a pale, golden wine with great delicacy and an aromatic bouquet. It needs to be consumed soon after purchase, or it will fade.

Fitou *(France)* Good, muscular red wine from the Languedoc-Roussillon area. It is among the best of the reds of the district and given time in bottle, it can become round and mellow.

Fixin *(France)* An important commune of the Côte de Nuits, making fine-quality red Burgundy. Vineyards of note include Clos de la Perrière and Clos du Chapitre.

Flagey-Échezeaux *(France)* Important red wine township in the Côte de Nuits with two front-ranking vineyards, Échezeaux and Grands Échezeaux. The first produces a fine rich, round wine and the second, which is not a single vineyard but a group, is also capable of producing fine wines but, like other divided properties, the quality of its wine is variable. The lesser wines of Flagey-Échezeaux are entitled to the appellation Vosne-Romanée.

Flaschengärung *(Germany)* This term, meaning bottle fermentation, may be used for a sparkling wine produced by the *méthode champenoise*.

Fleurie *(France)* One of the finest of the nine leading growths of the red wine Beaujolais area. A very stylish wine, with great fruitiness and bouquet. It tends to be one of the heavier wines of the Beaujolais area.

flute Tall, slender and elegantly shaped glass in which Champagne or other sparkling wines can be served more advantageously than in the old-style saucer-shaped glass. The flute retains the bubbles better than the open saucer shape, which lets them escape in a short time.

Forst *(Germany)* Celebrated wine-producing centre in the Rheinpfalz region making distinctive and very stylish wines chiefly from the Riesling grape. As a result of geological peculiarities in the district, the ground retains the sun's heat after nightfall, returning it to the vines and enabling them to produce grapes that are in a completely ripened condition. In consequence, the growers are able to make a fair quantity of German 'special category' wines, such as Beerenauslese. The most famous estate is the Jesuitengarten; others include Kirchenstück and Elster.

fortified wine This means any wine that has been strengthened by the addition of spirit, nearly always brandy. This is done, in some instances, simply to produce a stronger wine. In the case of port, it is a normal part of the production process. The addition of spirit during the period of fermentation arrests the fermentation development with the result that sugar in the fermenting must is not converted into alcohol but remains in the wine. This accounts for the sweetness of port.

Sherry, Madeira, Marsala and Malaga are other examples of fortified wines.

frais *(French)* Literally this means 'fresh', but on a bottle label it means 'chilled'. Thus *servir très frais* is 'serve well chilled'.

France The vineyards of France produce some twenty per cent of the world's wines, and the country is the foremost producer of quality wines, red, white, rosé and sparkling, as well as some fortified wines of special merit. Only a very small proportion of total output, however, falls within the general category of fine wine. Estimates put this proportion at around ten per cent of the annual production. The rest range from plain wines for everyday consumption to good-quality wines which are becoming increasingly popular in export markets as the price of the finer growths steadily rises.

Legal controls over authenticity and quality are stringent. They protect the names of individual vineyards and of the wines of a whole region. The protection is against 'passing off' inferior wines as those with a good reputation, a practice which was once rife in France and not completely unheard of, despite the controls, in recent years. In addition to protecting placenames, the controls go some way towards ensuring a reasonable standard of quality by setting down requirements for the production of protected wines. These include specifying the grape varieties that are used, the degree of alcoholic strength a wine must attain and, to prevent over-production, the maximum annual output of vineyards. These are the *appellation contrôlée* laws. While because of variations in vintage they cannot guarantee that every wine permitted to bear these words will be of a consistently high quality from year to year, they amount to a guarantee by the French government that such wine will be authentic and not faked in any way.

Improvements in overall standards continue to be achieved. Many of the smaller producers have formed co-operatives, which have the resources to invest in modern vinicultural and cellar equipment, to the benefit of the ultimate product. Government stations provide general guidance and technical advice and in some areas, which have traditionally concentrated on the production of low-quality wine from inferior but high-yielding grapes, there has been extensive replanting with better varieties. None of these developments has eradicated low-grade wine, and almost certainly never will, but they are helping to raise standards so that some areas which never had a market for their wines outside France now have a growing export business.

French skills in the art of viniculture are universally recognized and are unsurpassed elsewhere. The French *vigneron* has made his mark in various wine-producing countries throughout the world, among them Chile, the Rioja district of northern Spain, Africa and California.

There are scores of French placenames with a place in the world's wine gazetteer, ranging from tiny plots making only a few hundred cases each year to the large regions with a production of millions of gallons. The most famous are Bordeaux, Burgundy, Champagne, Alsace, Rhône and Loire. Many of them have districts that are just as well known; the districts contain notable parishes, and parishes may have one or more individual properties of world renown.

Franconia, Franken *(Germany)* One of the eleven officially designated wine regions of Germany, with wines being increasingly imported by the UK. The Müller-Thurgau grape predominates, nearly half the grape-growing areas using this vine. The Sylvaner comes second and the noble Riesling a long way behind. Unusually, for

Germany, many of the better wines are pressed from the Sylvaner. None, from whatever grape variety, is typically German; the wines tend to be light, fresh and quite dry, sometimes with an earthy flavour.

The term *Steinwein* has traditionally been applied in the UK to all Franconian wines, but under German wine law this term is restricted to an outstanding vineyard site in the city of Würzburg. Another peculiarly Franconian characteristic among German wines is that it has its own distinctive bottle – a flat flask, known as the *Bocksbeutel*.

Würzburg is the capital of the province, and the main wine centre. Other important localities are Escherndorf, Randersacker, Iphofen and Rödelsee.

Frascati *(Italy)* An attractive white wine made in the town of Frascati in the Alban Hills, south of Rome. It is full-bodied and fragrant, with a good golden colour. Though usually dry, a medium sweet style is also produced.

frizzante *(Italy)* The term for wine of any colour – red, white or rosé – that has a slight sparkle. Many such wines are sweet or sweetish. The best-known kind is Lambrusco.

Fronsac *(France)* A district of Bordeaux making full, soft, dark-coloured red wines, generally of sound quality. Appellations are Côtes Canon Fronsac and Côtes de Fronsac.

Frontignan *(France)* Town in the Languedoc-Roussillon area renowned for its sweet, golden dessert wine, normally fortified. It has the full, perfumed bouquet and flavour of the Muscat grape.

fruit wines Strictly, these are not wines at all, unless the fruit from which they are made is the grape. But a large number of fruits such as elderberry, apple and pear are used in the UK to make 'wine'. Some can be agreeable, sometimes bearing a faint resemblance to grape-based wines.

Furmint Superior white grape variety of Hungary, notable as the main constituent of Tokay, the famous sweet white wine of that country. Other white wines, agreeable but of lesser distinction, are made from the grape and some are marketed under its name.

Gaillac *(France)* City and district near Toulouse. This is an ancient source of wine for the English market, now back in favour as a result of the rising prices of wines from better known areas. The wines are full-bodied whites, dry and sweet. Some of them are made into sweet sparkling wine.

Gamay A grape variety, giving its name to a number of red wines of varying quality, but chiefly known as the great vine of the Beaujolais district of France. Here it produces a wine of much fame but of relatively small importance, though the wines of Beaujolais, at their best, can attain some distinction.

Gattinara *(Italy)* One of the foremost red wines of Italy, made from the Nebbiolo grape grown round the town of Gattinara in Piedmont. It is big-bodied, with a massive depth of flavour and a superb fragrance. Gattinara needs up to ten years to attain complete maturity, becoming sleek and rounded.

Gay-Lussac *(France)* This term appears occasionally on a French wine label or on a specialist merchant's list and refers to a system for measuring the strength of alcoholic beverages. The name is taken from the French chemist who devised it.

generic wines Wines that are sold under broad

or relatively broad geographical placenames, for example Bordeaux Rouge, Médoc and St-Julien. Such wines would be expected to show the general characteristics of the products of that area, but they will never be as fine as the wines from a narrowly defined place of origin. The practice of borrowing other countries' placenames, such as Californian Sauternes, is on the wane.

German Federal Republic Despite the ubiquitous slender brown and green bottles of Rhine and Moselle wines on the UK market, Germany is a comparatively small producer. Grape cultivation, even though it has spanned more than 2000 years, is a risky and fragile business, as well as an arduous one. The vineyards, often situated on steep slopes of stone and slate, are among the most northerly in Europe, with the risk of calamitous weather conditions always present. Yet austere terrain and an adverse climate are what great vines thrive on, and Germany is undoubtedly the producer of some of the world's finest wines.

Like France, Germany has customarily named wines after the location in which they are made, but it is noteworthy that the grape variety is of supreme importance and the German *vigneron* will often identify it on his label – especially if it is the

Riesling, a small, unprepossessing grape, with a low yield of juice, but which is the noble grape of Germany. Other important varieties are the Müller-Thurgau, a cross between the Riesling and the Sylvaner, the Sylvaner itself, the Ruländer and the Scheurebe.

There is some production of red wine, but its quality is not outstanding and it is available only in small quantities on the UK market. To all intents and purposes, from the viewpoint of British consumers, Germany is a white wine producer.

New German wine laws came into force with the 1971 vintage. They set down three grades of wine: *Tafelwein*, *Qualitätswein*, and *Qualitätswein mit Prädikat* and the last grade has six categories of special distinction. The law defines eleven wine-producing regions. Those that have significance on the UK market are Rheingau, Rheinhessen, Rheinpfalz (or Palatinate), Nahe, Mosel-Saar-Ruwer (officially three regions, but because of the general similarity of their wines, commonly lumped together), Franconia and Baden.

German placenames The majority, even the most famous, are villages or hamlets which would be unknown but for the quality of the wine they produce. Most of the renowned villages lie on south-facing slopes, engaging the sun all day long throughout the spring, summer and autumn to make their grapes riper and the wine they yield more fruity and fuller in flavour. The suffix 'er' is added to the names of towns and villages, giving Oppenheimer (a wine from Oppenheim) or Niersteiner (a wine from Nierstein), a practice uncommon in the UK but familiar when applied to human beings – thus, a Londoner.

Gevrey-Chambertin *(France)* Notable red wine commune of the Côte de Nuits with several illustrious vineyards including Le Chambertin, Chambertin-Clos de Bèze, Charmes-Chambertin and Latricières-Chambertin.

Gewürztraminer The great grape of Alsace which is also cultivated in other parts of the world. At its best it makes wine with an aromatic, spicy flavour, and wines pressed from this grape in Alsace are, in their style, unsurpassed anywhere else in the wine-producing world.

Ghemme *(Italy)* Village in Piedmont making a good full dry red wine from the Nebbiolo grape. Both the wine and grape are known locally as Spanna. Nearby villages making wine of the same style are Fara and Sizzano.

Gigondas *(France)* District of the Rhône region where good, full, beefy reds, typical of the robust Rhône style, are made. Rosé wine is also produced. It is agreeable but not of outstanding merit and must be consumed young.

Gironde *(France)* Department of France in which lie the great wine fields of Bordeaux.

Givry A commune of the Côte Chalonnaise making red and white wines of average quality for the area.

Glühwein *(Germany/Austria)* Hot, sweetened, spiced wine: a speciality in ski resorts.

Graach *(Germany)* Notable wine-producing district of the Mosel region, and located in the best-rated area, the Mittel-Mosel. The wines made here are among the lightest and sprightliest of the whole Mosel region. Famous vineyards include Himmelreich.

Graves *(France)* A large section of the Bordeaux region and producer of red and white wines, some of world-wide renown and most of the others of sound quality. The best of the white wines are dry, often high in alcohol, and sold under château names; they are fruity, crisp and firm. Lesser wines, sold as Graves or Graves Supérieures, may be dry, semi–dry or semi–sweet, and can make amenable drinking. The red wines of Graves, considerably outnumbered by the whites, have a delicate nose, considerable depth, and a fine, limpid ruby colour. The best are compared with some of the finer wines of Médoc, but in general they lack the finesse of Médocs. Whites are made mainly from the Sauvignon Blanc and Sémillon grapes, reds mainly from the Cabernet. The best communes are Pessac, Léognan, Martillac, Talence and Cadaujac. Plainer styles of Graves include Graves de Vayres and Graves Supérieures.

Graves Supérieures *(France)* An appellation for white wines from the Graves district. Like other 'superior' designations, under French law it is superior only to the lowest-ranking appellation, not to the best. It will be of rather better quality and of higher alcoholic strength than plain white Graves or Bordeaux Blanc.

Graves de Vayres *(France)* Enclave of Graves making red and white wine and accorded its own appellation. Vayres is the main village. The reds are good, round wines, quick to mature; the whites are round and flavoursome. They are above the general standard of plain Graves but are not to be compared with the better growths of the district.

Great Plain, The *(Hungary)* An immensely prolific wine-producing area of Hungary, in which vines were planted to reclaim the land from sand left by the Danube; the wines are thus commonly known as 'sand wines'. The popular Hungarian varieties of grape, the Kadarka and the Olasz Riesling, are cultivated here, producing wines that are acceptable but of little distinction. A familiar label name is linked to that of the town of Kecskemét, Kecskeméti Olasz Riesling.

Greece Ancient home of wine, and still a significant producer, but of minor importance in the UK. A number of retailers stock Retsina, which is a Greek speciality. Much wine is made from the Muscat grape, and is richly sweet and highly perfumed. Among dry wines, the reds are in general more satisfactory than the whites, which tend to have the earthy, scorched flavour common to wines produced in hot climates. The most acceptable light wines, for British tastes, are the reds and whites produced by the firms of Achaia-Clauss under the brand name Demestica and Andrew Cambas, brand name Hymettus.

Grenache Adaptable red grape variety, responsible for some of the best red wines of Châteauneuf-du-Pape and for some of the better rosé wines of Tavel. The Grenache is also used to make sweet wines in southern France, notably Banyuls, where it is known as the Alicante. It is also an important grape in the Rioja region of northern Spain.

Gris, Vin An extremely pale pink wine.

Groslot *(France)* Secondary red wine grape variety. It is cultivated extensively in the Loire valley where it makes the plainer styles of the rather sweet Rosé d'Anjou. Also grown elsewhere in France, it produces a fairly plain red wine.

Growth A vineyard or district of vineyards, equivalent to the French word *cru*. Thus 'first growth' is equivalent to *premier cru* and 'classified growth' to *cru classé*.

Gumpoldskirchen *(Austria)* One of Austria's best known white wine towns in the Baden area near Vienna, making light, fresh, dry wines from such grapes as the Grüner Veltliner or Riesling. Sweeter styles, e.g. Spätlese and Auslese wines, are also made.

Hallgarten *(Germany)* Town in the Rheingau region with high-lying vineyards that make extremely stylish, full-bodied wines in a good year, but perform, on average, less well than many other Rheingau vineyards in years in which weather conditions have been unsatisfactory.

Hattenheim *(Germany)* A village of the Rheingau region surrounded by vineyards. Part of the renowned Markobrunn vineyard lies within its boundaries, but these wines are now designated Erbacher Markobrunn, after the neighbouring village of Erbach. Hattenheim has its own renowned vineyard, Steinberg, notable for its fairly light but remarkably scented wines, and other top-quality wines are made and sold under the Hattenheimer label.

Haut-Médoc *(France)* The finest part of the Médoc region of Bordeaux, and the location of all the region's famous vineyards. Any wine carrying the appellation Haut-Médoc will be of superior quality to one with the simple appellation Médoc.

Hermitage *(France)* A famous red and white wine district of the Rhône region. The reds are vigorous, strong, solid-bodied wines which can, with cask and bottle age, achieve considerable finesse. They are likely to form a bottle sediment and therefore need to be decanted. The white wines of Hermitage, made in smaller quantities than the red, are dry and refined in flavour, but have good body and an assertive bouquet. They are long-lived and will mellow in bottle.

Hochheim *(Germany)* Important wine centre of the Rheingau region, producing wines that are not always typical of the region. In a good year, however, they are undoubtedly wines of fine quality.

Hock *(Germany)* The generic name for wine originating in the Rhineland of Germany. The word is thought to be a corruption of the placename Hochheim, an important centre in the Rheingau region, and has certainly been in use in Britain since the Victorian era, when German white wines became popular following their patronage by Queen Victoria and the Royal family.

Hospices de Beaune *(France)* An ancient charity, founded in 1443, providing a home for the elderly and needy in Beaune, Burgundy. The institution derives its income from the sale of the wine from the many vineyards in its possession, which have been bequeathed to the Hospices de Beaune over the centuries. In November of each year the wines from the various vineyards are sold by auction in Beaune, and this annual sale tends to set the level for Burgundy prices generally.

Hospices de Beaune wines may be red or white, and several of them come from highly rated properties. The labels bear the names of the individual benefactors. Although they come mainly from good vineyards, there is no reason why, at the retail end of the market, they should be expected to command higher prices than those for other noted vineyards anywhere else in Burgundy.

House wine Any wine that is sold by bottle, carafe or glass in restaurants or hotels. Normally this is the least expensive wine on the restaurant list, except for carafe wine, but is not necessarily the worst.

Huelva *(Spain)* A region producing heavy, white wines, the best of which can bear comparison with some grades of sherry or with Montilla.

Hungary Producer of Tokay, one of the world's greatest sweet white wines, and of Bull's Blood, one of the most colourfully named. Hungary is also a prolific producer of sound light wines in a variety of styles.

Production standards are of a very high order and some distinctive grape varieties are grown: Furmint, Ezerjó, Olasz Riesling and Keknyelü, among the whites; Kadarka and Kékfrankos among the reds. Apart from Tokay, the main production areas are Eger, Balaton, Pécs, the Great Plain, Sopron and Mór. Hungarian wine names are a combination of the place of origin, with the addition of the letter 'i', and the grape variety, for example Soproni-Kékfrankos, Balatoni Olasz Riesling.

Iphofen (*Germany*) One of the better-rated communes of Franconia. Vineyard names of note include Julius Echterberg and Kronsberg.

Israel An ancient home of wine, but modern production of any significance started only in 1948, since when it has grown apace. Vineyard areas are scattered and placenames are of small importance on the British market. The reds, whites, rosés and dessert wines are sold under brand names, often accompanied by the name of the grape variety used. These include some of the more prolific, and therefore lesser, French varieties, as well as some of the noble grapes of France, such as Cabernet Sauvignon and Sémillon.

The wines are, in general, well made, and often represent good value, but none is of outstanding merit.

Italy The world's largest producer of wine, accounting for about one-fifth of all output. It is also a considerable producer of vermouth. Light wines are sometimes sold under the name of the grape variety they are made from, for example Sangiovese, sometimes under the name of the village or town or district in which they are made, such as Valpolicella, or sometimes under a combination of grape variety and placename as with Verdicchio dei Castelli di Jesi. Italian light wine covers virtually every conceivable style, from fresh clean young whites such as Soave to dark solid reds like Barolo. There is also extensive production of sparkling wines, of which Asti Spumante is the best known, and of dessert wines, Marsala being the outstanding example.

Among the better light wines, reds almost always offer best value for money. Some wines, like Lacrima Christi, are more celebrated for their names than for their quality.

Since 1963, when Italy introduced laws to control the use of placenames, the overall quality of wine has significantly improved and exports have steadily increased.

The important regions, in terms of quality wines, are Campania, Emilia-Romagna, Latium, Lombardy, Marche, Piedmont, Sardinia, Sicily, Trentino-Alto Adige, Tuscany, Umbria and Veneto.

Jaune, Vin *(France)* A yellow-coloured wine made in the Jura and having some of the general characteristics of sherry. The finest wine of this style comes from Château-Chalon.

Jerez *(Spain)* City of Andalucia in southern Spain and the centre of the sherry industry. The word 'sherry' is a corruption of the name Jerez.

Johannisberg *(Germany)* Tiny white wine-producing village of the Rheingau region. Its proudest possession is the Schloss Johannisberg, a prime estate making great, weighty wine, unsurpassed elsewhere in the Rheingau, and commanding some of the highest prices of any German wine. There are other good vineyards entitled to the Johannisberger name but German wine law has extended the official area so that Johannisberg is no longer a totally dependable appellation. The wines, though, are generally of satisfactory quality.

Johannisberger *(Switzerland)* see **Valais**

Juliénas *(France)* One of the nine principal red wine communes of the Beaujolais area. Although it has the privilege of being allowed to link its own name with the Beaujolais appellation, its wines may fairly be described as middle-of-the-road among the better wines of the area, but they have the good Beaujolais characteristics – light, fruity, and flowery. Juliénas is a wine that will last, retaining these characteristics for two or three years, but it is not the most outstanding of the nine communes.

Jura *(France)* Mountainous vineyard area producing a range of red, white and rosé wines, as well as the uncommon *vins jaunes* ('yellow' wines) and *vins de paille* ('straw' wines). The three superior appellations are Arbois, Château-Chalon and L'Étoile.

Jurançon *(France)* A golden, sweet, slightly spicy wine made in the foothills of the Pyrenees from grape varieties not encountered elsewhere. The wine acquires great fragrance and mellowness with bottle age. The area also produces dry white wines, for early consumption. They are not outstanding.

Kabinett *(Germany)* A distinction in the grading quality under German wine laws. Wine qualifying for this term will be made from grapes harvested at the normal time but which will be judged by the authorities to be of above-average quality. The expectation of a *Kabinett* wine, therefore, is that it will be among the better qualities of German wine.

Kadarka Red wine grape variety of Hungary, used in the production of the majority of the country's better red wines. Notable among them is Villány Kadarka and Bull's Blood. Depending upon the vinification process, the Kadarka can yield wines of considerable depth and substance.

Kaiserstuhl *(Germany)* District of the Baden region producing on volcanic soil some of the best wines of the region with a tendency to be big-bodied and fruity. The grape that produces the best results is the Ruländer, or Pinot Gris. Villages of special note include Ihringen and Achkarren.

Kéknyelü A white grape variety of Hungary. The most notable of the wines pressed from it come from the Badacsony area.

Kir *(France)* White wine flavoured with Crème

de Cassis, a blackcurrant liqueur or, more economically, blackcurrant cordial. The recipe calls for a dash of liqueur or cordial in a wine glass, topped up with inexpensive dry white wine, well chilled. Some wine merchants offer pre-mixed Kir.

Lacrima Christi *(Italy)* Red and white wines made on the slopes of Mount Vesuvius near Naples. The name – sometimes appearing as Lacryma Cristi – is well known in the British market, but only for whites, which can be dry or semi-sweet. This is an agreeable wine but of no special merit.

Lago di Caldaro *(Italy)* One of the better red wines from the Trentino-Alto Adige region. It is light, fragrant and easy to drink.

Lalande de Pomerol *(France)* Red wine district of Bordeaux, adjoining the important Pomerol area. The wines compare well with average Pomerols, though not with the better growths. The notable property is Château Bel-Air.

La Mancha *(Spain)* A sprawling area of central Spain, with a prolific output. It embraces a great range of wines, few of which have any special merit, though few of those exported to the UK market can be described as utterly bad. The area produces a great deal of wine destined for export. In the UK it will usually show up as 'Spanish Full Red', or 'Spanish Dry White', names such as 'Spanish Burgundy' or 'Spanish Chablis' now being prohibited under EEC regulations. The area is, in short, a producer of low-priced wines, but recently there have been signs that growers want a more dignified slice of the export trade, and some are prepared to improve their quality to meet this requirement. So far, however, few indications of this ambition are showing through.

Lambrusco *(Italy)* Slightly sparkling red wine, made from the grape of the same name in Northern Italy. It has a generous fruity bouquet and is full-flavoured, though rather sweet. Lambrusco has scored a considerable success on the United States market, but has not done so well in Britain, although it is readily available.

Languedoc-Roussillon *(France)* An immense area running along the Mediterranean. Traditionally a major source of *Vins ordinaires*, but in recent years showing a distinct improvement in quality, partly as a result of the interest and investment of important French wine interests, partly to the settlement in the region of skilled *vignerons* from ex-colonial territories in North Africa.

Wines of many styles are made, and quality is variable. Districts for light wines of particular merit include Costières du Gard, St-Chinian, Faugères, Corbières and Minervois, but there are several others which have a place in the category of VDQS. The area is also known for a number of sweet, fortified wines (*Vins de liqueur*), the best known of which are Banyuls and Frontignan.

Latium *(Italy)* A region producing two of Italy's best-known wines, Frascati and Est! Est!! Est!!!

laying down 'Wines for laying down' is a term frequently encountered in the lists of better retailers. In this context it applies mainly to claret, Burgundy and port, and the inference is that wines so categorized are too young to drink until they have lain in bottle for some years.

Laying down requires certain conditions, especially concerning the temperature of the place in which the wines are to be laid, and few houses in the UK are equipped with cellars in which the proper conditions exist. But a wine merchant offering such wines is likely to have cellars, in which he will keep customers' wines for a fee.

Léognan *(France)* A celebrated commune of

Graves producing red and white wine. Among its important properties are Châteaux Carbonnieux, Olivier, Haut-Bailly and the Domaine de Chevalier.

lees A deposit or sediment remaining in the bottle or cask.

Lessona *(Italy)* A good, full-flavoured red, made in Piedmont from the best red wine grape in Italy, the Nebbiolo. A similarity to Gattinara is discernible, but Lessona is not in the same class.

L'Étoile *(France)* One of the three principal districts of the Jura area. It makes good white wines of a fairly high standard, some of which are made into sparkling wines.

Libourne *(France)* An important centre of the Bordeaux wine trade. Wines from nearby districts are known locally as Libournais, and include St-Émilion, Pomerol and Fronsac.

Liebfraumilch *(Germany)* A white blended wine with the general characteristics of Rhine wine. German wine law requires that a Liebfraumilch must be made with Riesling, Sylvaner or Müller-Thurgau grapes from the regions of Rheinhessen,

Nahe, Rheinpfalz or Rheingau. It is classified as a *Qualitätswein*.

light wines Under EEC regulations these are legally defined as wines that are unfortified, or naturally made. Claret, Burgundy, hock and Moselle are examples. In Britain they were formerly called table wines. 'Light', however, is also a wine taster's term for wines that are not full or medium bodied. They are usually fresh-tasting wines, probably of low alcoholic strength.

Lillet *(France)* The brand name of an aperitif based on Bordeaux white wine and fortified with Armagnac brandy.

Liquore *(France)* A naturally sweet, rich white wine.

Lirac *(France)* A village in the Rhône valley, known for its rosé wines. It is close to the famous rosé wine village of Tavel and its wines are of a comparable character, though they tend to be somewhat lighter-bodied.

Listrac *(France)* A red and white wine commune of the Haut-Médoc district of Bordeaux with reds predominating. Some of the wine is entitled to the appellation of Moulis; other wines carry the name of the commune. The reds are sturdy and well flavoured.

Loire Valley *(France)* An immensely long thin stretch of vineyards running from the Massif Central to the Bay of Biscay, a distance of about 483 km (300 miles). The wines are therefore considerably varied, but several are of extremely good quality and have found a ready marketplace in the UK since the astronomic rise in the price of French wines from more traditional sources began some 20 years ago. The area produces red, white and rosé and sparkling wines, of varying quality. Names of importance are Anjou, Coteaux de la Loire, Coteaux du Layon, Pouilly-sur-Loire, Touraine, Quincy, Reuilly, Sancerre, Savennières, Saumur, Chinon, Bourgueil, and Vouvray, and important grapes of the area are the Muscadet and the Gros Plant.

Lombardy *(Italy)* An important wine-producing region, with the red Valtellina one of its outstanding wines.

Loupiac *(France)* Village on the River Garonne, facing the Sauternes commune of Barsac and producing, in a good year when the grapes have sufficiently ripened, sweet white wines of a kind comparable to those of Barsac, though never with the depth and distinction of wines from the better Barsac properties.

Ludon *(France)* Commune of the Haut-Médoc. Its most important claret is made at Château La Lagune, a vineyard among the third growths of the Médoc.

Lussac-St-Émilion *(France)* Bordeaux red wine commune in the vicinity of St-Émilion and with the right to join the St-Émilion appellation to its name. The wines are generally full-bodied but of no great distinction.

Lutomer, or Ljutomer *(Yugoslavia)* Best-known district of Slovenia. See **Yugoslavia**.

Luxembourg The Grand Duchy of Luxembourg has a stretch of the northern bank of the Moselle river running for some 32 km (20 miles). This is where the vineyards lie, producing white wines that are light, crisp and fairly tart, not unlike the lighter styles from the Moselle region of Germany. The Elbling grape, not notable as a producer of good wine, is widely grown, but much land is also under the Riesling. Luxembourg also makes sparkling wines, among which there are some of special merit.

Macau *(France)* Village of the Haut-Médoc with an important property, Château Cantemerle, making claret of outstanding quality.

Mâcon, Mâconnais *(France)* Town and district in the south of the Burgundy region which is a large source of red and white wines. Much of it is plain wine, sold as Mâcon Rouge or Blanc, of which the latter is likely to be the more satisfactory, light and crisply dry. Some wine of similar calibre is sold as Pinot-Chardonnay-Mâcon. A slightly higher grade is Mâcon Supérieur, while wine entitled to the appellation Mâcon-Villages and those using a village name will be of better quality. But the best and best known wines of the area, all white, are Pouilly-Fuissé, Saint-Véran, Pouilly-Loché, Pouilly-Vinzelles, and Viré.

made wine The EEC technical term for wine which has been fermented from the juice of grapes which have been imported, either whole or in concentrated form.

Madeira Fortified wine, mostly sweet though some is dry, taking its name from the Portuguese island of Madeira off the coast of north-west Africa. The wine has had a high reputation for some four centuries. Originally an extremely slow-maturing wine, it was discovered that a long sea journey would speed up maturity. Later it was found that heating the wine for a prolonged period had the same result, and since then one part of the process of making Madeira has been to keep it at a high temperature in heated rooms called *estufas* for several months. It is this part of the process that gives Madeira its attractive 'roast' flavour. The producers use the solera system of the sherry producers, and occasionally a bottle will show the date of the inception of the solera. Vintage Madeira was once made but is now a rarity.

Madeira is a remarkably long-lived wine; in bottle it will keep indefinitely, and even in a bottle that has been opened it will last for several months. The four main styles, which take their names from the grape they are made from, are Sercial, the driest; Verdelho, medium-sweet; Bual, sweet; and Malmsey, lusciously sweet. Rainwater is a less common, light style.

magnum A bottle that has twice the capacity of a standard bottle. It is often used for Champagne and sometimes also for Burgundy, claret and occasionally even sherry. A magnum of Champagne is likely to cost more than the price of two standard bottles, largely because of the high breakage rate in Champagne producers' cellars. Red wine in magnums will mature more slowly than the same wine in a standard bottle, so that the optimum opening time for a magnum is likely to be two years or so after the time suggested by vintage charts, which apply to standard-sized bottles.

Malaga *(Spain)* A dark-coloured dessert wine from Andalucia. The grapes are partially dried in the sun, giving the wine a strong, raisin-like flavour.

Malbec A variety of red grape widely grown in Bordeaux (France) and elsewhere in that country. In Bordeaux it is one of the primary constituents of claret.

Malmsey *(Portugal)* The sweetest style of Madeira, rich, luscious and full. It is one of the world's finest dessert wines.

Manzanilla *(Spain)* A very dry Fino sherry which has been matured in bodegas near the sea, acquiring from the sea air a distinctive salty tang.

Like other Finos it will not keep indefinitely and should be consumed very soon after purchase.

Marche *(Italy)* Province on the Adriatic coast. Its best-known wine is the straw-coloured white Verdicchio, made from the grape of the same name.

Margaux *(France)* A celebrated commune of the Bordeaux area of Haut-Médoc. It is singular among the foremost communes of Médoc in that most of its vineyards produce claret that is all of a distinctly high standard and typical of the overall character of the wine of the commune. Generally lighter than the wines of other Médoc communes, it has a distinctive bouquet, a smooth texture and outstanding finesse.

The most famous property is Château Margaux, a first growth; second growth châteaux include Rausan-Ségla, Rauzan-Gassies and Brane-Cantenac. The villages of Cantenac, Soussans, Arsac and Labarde are also entitled to the Margaux appellation.

Marino *(Italy)* A white, dry wine after the style of Frascati.

Marque *(France)* The term *Marque deposée* means

that the trade name has been registered.

Marsala *(Italy)* Best-known fortified dessert wine of Italy, named after the town in Sicily which is the centre of the trade. The wine was 'discovered' by an Englishman, John Woodhouse, in the late 1700s and Lord Nelson later ordered 500 casks of it for his Mediterranean Fleet.

Marsala is a minor member of the league of fortified wines marketed in Europe. For the most part it is a rich wine with a burnt flavour; Marsala Superiori is among the most distinctive styles. A dry variety, Marsala Vergini, is also made, though the heaviness of the basic wine does not put it on a par with the more delicate styles of sherry or even Madeira.

Marsala Speciali has Marsala as its base and is flavoured with various ingredients, of which the best-known version in Britain is Marsala All'uovo, with egg. Other additions include quinine and almonds.

Marsannay *(France)* Village of Burgundy making a good rosé wine from the noble Pinot Noir grape. It is light, fresh and fruity, and is one of the better rosé wines of France.

Martillac *(France)* A commune of Graves noted

for its excellent red wines. The best-known property is Château Smith-Haut-Lafitte. Good white wines are also produced.

mature, maturity A state reached by wine – usually, but not necessarily, red – in which it has reached the prime of its development. Very light red wines and the majority of white wines are already mature when they are bought, and need no further ageing in bottle. But some wines are offered by comprehensive wine merchants while they are still too young for drinking, and are usually at a price that reflects this unreadiness. Those who buy young wines can do so at a price advantage but must be prepared to make room in their homes to store such wines away for a few years, until they are mature. This requires proper wine-storage conditions (see **Cellarage**). Alternatively, some merchants will make space available for laying down customers' wines, but will charge an annual fee for doing so. This may well cancel out any saving achieved by buying immature wines, although inflation may make it still worth while.

Good-quality clarets and Burgundies are among red wines that, coming from a recent good vintage, will need time to mature in bottle, as will the best of the Rhône reds. Some white wines, although probably mature at the time of purchase, can attain a finer state of maturity if kept in bottle for a few years. They include the better growths of Sauternes and of vintage Champagne. But of all categories of wines, the one that is likely to be most advantageous to the consumer if set aside for a few years is Vintage port.

Mavrodaphne *(Greece)* An ancient red wine grape stock, peculiar to Greece, where it makes a dessert wine of the same name. Traditionally the maturing casks are left out in the sunshine for several years, and the wine becomes increasingly concentrated. Mavrodaphne is normally of high alcoholic strength.

Maximin Grünhaus *(Germany)* An outstanding estate of the Ruwer region, making fresh, delicate wines which are at their best in a vintage preceded by a long period of dry weather.

Médoc *(France)* Premier area of Bordeaux, making the greatest proportion of fine red wines of any area in the world. They are highly prized and, among the better growths, highly priced. The Médoc contains more than half the famous red wine châteaux of Bordeaux; among them are such celebrated names as Château Lafite, Château

Margaux, Château Latour and Château Mouton-Rothschild. Not surprisingly, since great wines are invariably made in difficult circumstances, the soil is generally of absurdly poor quality, mostly sand, silt and gravel with patches of clay. A lot of the land is marshy, since a large area has for centuries been under water or lapped by water. Its name spells out the character of the terrain: conjured up by the Romans, it was originally *in medio aquae* – which means literally in the middle of the water.

The northern part of the Médoc is the least well endowed in terms of fine wine. It is from here that many of the plainer wines bearing the simple 'Médoc' appellation come. The finest wines are made in the part of the area known as Haut-Médoc, within the boundaries of which lie the most important parishes, St-Estèphe, Pauillac, St-Julien and Margaux, distinguished by the quality of their wines. Bottles bearing these names can be expected to contain wine of considerable superiority to anything that may be labelled simply 'Médoc', and some occasionally outclass the wines from the lesser-known châteaux of the district. But in general it is the wines of the known châteaux, and especially the classified growths, that are the finest.

Little white wine is made, and it is not permitted, under French wine law, to carry the name 'Médoc'.

Mercurey *(France)* Wine parish of the Côte Chalonnaise and the best and best-known centre for red wines in the area. They are relatively light, for early consumption, but often have remarkable fruitiness and a certain elegance and can represent good value for money. A small quantity of white wine is also made, though it is of a lesser standard than the reds.

Merlot An ordinary red wine grape producing, in its own right, wines of no particular distinction, but very useful in the Médoc (France) to give an overall softness to a blend of grape varieties. It is also grown elsewhere, for example in Italy and the United States, and increasingly sold under its varietal name. As such, it is a light-bodied, fairly full-tasting wine of small character.

Messa, Vino da *(Italy)* Sacramental wine, made according to Church requirements.

méthode champenoise *(France)* A painstaking, laborious, labour-intensive and costly production process used by Champagne makers and others elsewhere in France and various other countries in the preparation of sparkling wine. The words may appear on the labels of sparkling wines from outside the Champagne region, and this is an indication that the wine has been made by the process, rather than by more rapid and economical methods, and is therefore certainly likely to be a sparkling wine of good quality. But no wine outside the Champagne region may style itself 'Champagne', whether or not it has been made by the *méthode champenoise*.

Initially, the grape juice is fermented in casks or glass-lined vats to give a still, dry wine. In March, following the vintage, the wines are blended in the proportion that will produce the correct balance of quality and style. It is then bottled, after the addition of yeast and sugar, to promote a secondary fermentation within the bottle which creates the 'sparkle'. The wine is then corked and left to mature for several years.

This second fermentation does, however, develop sediment. To get rid of this the bottles are placed at an acute angle, neck downwards, in special racks. Each day skilled workmen turn the bottles in a rotary movement which brings the sediment gradually on to the cork, an operation known as *remuage*. *Dégorgement*, the next process, is the ejection of the sediment. The neck of the bottle is dipped into a refrigerating liquid so that a lump of ice forms around the cork, securing the sediment. The cork is then removed, and under the pressure of carbonic acid gas, the ice and sediment shoot out.

The wine should now be crystal clear, the fermentation in the bottle having consumed all the sugar. Each bottle is now topped up with the same wine and to it is generally added a sweetening agent – cane sugar – in varying proportion according to the type of Champagne required, mixed with a little brandy. This is known as *liqueur d'expédition*. Then the final cork is inserted, the wire fixed, and the bottle is labelled.

Meursault *(France)* Important white wine commune of the Côte de Beaune. The wine is dry and straw coloured, with a big body and a distinctive bouquet. Among the best vineyards are Les Perrières, Les Genevrières and Les Charmes. In general, the wines of less important vineyards in the commune are of high quality.

Minervois *(France)* One of the best-rated districts of the Languedoc-Roussillon area, especially for its reds, which tend to be robust wines with good balance.

Minho *(Portugal)* A region producing red, white

and rosé wines known as *vinhos verdes* or 'green' wines, because they are pressed from grapes that have not attained full maturity.

Mis en Bouteille au Château *(France)* Term meaning 'bottled in the vineyard of origin'; château bottled (CB). It may appear on the label, and is an indication of a wine's authenticity.

moelleux *(France)* A French term meaning, literally, 'marrow', though the word *moelleux* on a French label will almost certainly mean that the wine is sweet.

Monbazillac *(France)* Vineyard district close to Bergerac noted for its sound, sweet white wines which have some affinity with those of Sauternes. Monbazillac is made from the same grapes as Sauternes (Sémillon with some Muscat) but tends to have a more pronounced Muscat flavour. The better wines can equal and sometimes surpass the cheaper styles of Sauternes.

monopole *(France)* A word which regularly occurs on French wine labels. It means no more than that the producer is claiming that the wine within the bottle is his monopoly, and therefore exclusive.

Montagne-Saint-Émilion *(France)* A red wine commune of Bordeaux, adjacent to the major vineyards of St-Émilion, and entitled to add the appellation to its name. The wines have some similarity to those of St-Émilion, but they are more solid and less refined. They make agreeable drinking at moderate cost.

Montagny *(France)* A commune of the Côte Chalonnaise concentrating on white wine, some of which is of very high quality, though it does not rank among the fine wines of Burgundy. The general run of white is not of especially high quality, but is an agreeable, light fresh dry wine for early drinking.

Montefiascione see **Est! Est!! Est!!!**

Montepulciano *(Italy)* Splendid hill town in Tuscany producing a sound, full-flavoured red wine from the Sangiovese grape.

Montilla *(Spain)* A sherry-like wine, though not permitted by law to be sold as sherry, made in the area of Montilla-Moriles, near Córdoba, southern Spain. Dry, medium and sweet versions are produced. It is seldom fortified, as sherry is, so making a lighter drink than sherry, and is especially suitable as a pre-lunch aperitif. The Amontillado style of sherry takes its name from Montilla.

Montlouis *(France)* A district of the Loire region producing sound white wines, usually semi-sweet, from the Chenin grape. Some are *pétillant*. Montlouis turns some of its production into sparkling wine.

Montrachet see **Chassagne-Montrachet and Puligny-Montrachet**

Mór *(Hungary)* District close to Budapest producing a dry, golden, full-flavoured wine from the Ezerjó grape, marketed as Móri Ezerjó.

Morey-Saint-Denis *(France)* A commune in the Côte de Nuits possessing a number of distinguished red wine vineyards. Among them are Clos de Tart, Clos de la Roche, and part of Les Bonnes Mares – the other part is in the commune of Chambolle-Musigny.

Morgon *(France)* An important commune of the red-wine area of Beaujolais producing good wines which tend to be rather out of step with the reputation of Beaujolais as a lightish wine for drinking young. The products of this commune, though showing the broad characteristics of the area's wines, are shorter on fruit than many others. They are relatively full-bodied and will improve with bottle age, sometimes assuming a resemblance to one of the better red Burgundies.

Morocco *(North Africa)* As in Algeria and Tunisia, modern wine production was introduced by the French, and the country's wine traditions have benefited as a result. The best wines are red. Placenames are of small importance, and are unlikely to be shown on the labels of Moroccan wines available in the UK, which usually designate the wine simply as 'Moroccan', or sell it under a more prominent brand name.

Moroccan wines are inexpensive but can offer good value against those from southern France, which can often be more expensive and, by contrast, coarser. Wines from Morocco are often strong in alcohol.

Moselle, Mosel *(Germany)* Very notable region producing white wines, mainly from the Riesling grape, with an assertive, perfumed bouquet and a light, crisp flavour.

Mosel-Saar-Ruwer *(Germany)* The Mosel river

valley is the major area. The Saar and the Ruwer are tributaries running into it, while the Mosel itself is a tributary of the Rhine, which runs through the finest wine sites in Germany. But the Mosel district is in no way inferior to the Rhine as a producer of wines on the grand scale. Separately, the Mosel, Saar, and Ruwer are three of Germany's designated wine-producing regions. Along these rivers some of the world's most delicate white wines are made, the best of them from the Riesling grape.

Mosel wines are put into tall, slender, green-glass bottles, which distinguishes them from the wines of the Rhine, bottled in brown glass. The main districts are Piesport, Brauneberg, Bernkastel, Graach, Wehlen and Zeltingen, all of which lie in the best-rated area, the middle (or Mittel) Mosel; Wiltingen (on the Saar) and Maximin Grünhaus, on the Ruwer.

Moulin à Vent *(France)* Important commune of the Beaujolais area and widely regarded as the finest of the nine principal red wine communes of the area. Its wines are among the fullest in Beaujolais; they have a superb deep colour, a robust body and great breeding. Yet they also retain the unmistakable flowery character that has made Beaujolais renowned.

The wines of this commune are long-lasting by Beaujolais standards and will develop well in bottle over several years.

Moulis *(France)* A commune of small importance in the Haut-Médoc area, entitled to its own appellation but with no outstanding growths. It produces sound, well-made red wines at a moderate price.

Mousseux *(France)* The French term for sparkling wine. In France, all sparkling wines are so described, with the exception of Champagne, which is properly considered to have such high renown that the application of the word is unnecessary. The appellation laws recognize certain areas and districts as the source of sound sparkling wines, so that the words 'Mousseux de' may be used with such placenames as Bordeaux, Arbóis, L'Étoile, Bourgogne, Seysell, Saint-Péray, Saumur and Vouvray. Sparkling wines which cannot claim an appellation are sold under brand names.

mulled wine Heated red wine with the addition of such spices as nutmeg, cloves and cinnamon, sometimes lemon or orange peel, plus sugar and often spirits. Some recipes call for claret or port, but since the quality of the wine does not show through the other ingredients, cheaper wines of a similar style make the drink more economical.

Müller-Thurgau A white grape variety making soft, fairly short-lived wines. Grown extensively in Germany, it has also found favour elsewhere, including Alsace and England.

Muscadet *(France)* A grape variety performing at its best in the Loire Valley, France, and the best-known wine of the area. Typical Muscadet from the Loire is a light, dry, crisp wine. The best of it comes from the Sèvre and Maine region (Muscadet de Sèvre-et-Maine) and is likely to sell at a higher price than the general run of Muscadet. Other Loire districts cultivating the Muscadet grape do not, generally, show their name on the label.

Muscadet sur Lie see **sur lie**

Muscat, Muscadelle, Moscatello Members of a vast family of grapes, which may be white or black, grown in virtually all the world's wine-producing countries. They produce full, scented wines with a pronounced grapey flavour. Most are sweet, but Muscat wine from Alsace is dry. In

Bordeaux, as Muscadelle, it is used to add flavour to sweet white wines; in southern France, as Muscat, it makes heavy fortified wines such as Muscat de Beaumes-de-Venise, and in Italy, as Moscato, it makes Asti Spumante and numerous other wines usually prefixed Moscato.

Nackenheim *(Germany)* An outstanding area of the Rheinhessen region. It makes fruity, finely scented wines that are sometimes compared with the wines of the better-known area of Nierstein. Among the distinguished vineyards is Rothenberg.

Nahe *(Germany)* Valley of the River Nahe, a tributary of the Rhine. Nahe is one of the eleven officially designated wine-producing regions of Germany. The leading grape variety is Müller-Thurgau, followed by the Riesling and the Sylvaner. The general characteristics of Nahe wines lie somewhere between the light crispness of Moselles and the fullness of Rheingaus. As elsewhere in Germany, the Riesling grape is the basis of the most distinguished wines, and in the upper reaches of the Nahe valley it produces racy, fruity wines. The district with the highest reputation is Schloss Böckelheim. Other important districts include Bad Kreuznach, Rüdesheim (not to be confused with a district of the same name in the Rheingau region, where finer wines are produced), Niederhausen, Norheim and Roxheim.

Nasco *(Italy)* Strong white dessert wine, made in Sardinia. It has an unusual combination of fruit flavours and is, perhaps, one of Italy's dessert wines deserving wider recognition.

Nebbiolo Italy's most distinguished red grape variety, making big, long-lasting wines. The best-known names are Barolo, Barbaresco, Gattinara and Ghemme. Wine made from the grape in lesser districts is often under a name that embodies the name of the grape.

Nebuchadnezzar A giant bottle, holding the equivalent of 20 standard bottles.

négociant *(France)* A wine dealer with responsibilities over and above those of a dealer in any other kind of commodity. In Bordeaux, and especially in Burgundy, the *négociant* has to attend to the blending of wines, the bottling of them, and the shipping. He is responsible not only for the wines that he ships, but for their reputation, upon which his own reputation depends. See also **éleveur**.

Neuchâtel *(Switzerland)* A French-speaking canton of Switzerland, with extensive vineyards along the shores of Lake Neuchâtel. Whites are made from the Chasselas grape, known to the Swiss as the Fendant. They are light, dry, refreshing wines, though sometimes rather thin. Many are *pétillant*, and are described as 'star' wines. Rosé wine, known as Oeil de Perdrix, is also made, and so is Cortaillod, a good light-bodied, fruity red made from the Pinot Noir grape and taking its name from a village. Cortaillod is rated as the best red wine of Switzerland.

Niederhausen *(Germany)* This is a quite distinguished district in the Nahe region. Outstanding among its vineyards are Hermannshöhle and Rosenberg.

Nierstein *(Germany)* The most notable district of the Rheinhessen region giving its name to one of the best-known German wines, Niersteiner. All the finest wines are pressed from the Riesling grape. Hipping, Glöck and Bildstock are some of the best vineyard sites. An especially familiar name from the area is Niersteiner Gutes Domtal. This is not a single vineyard name, but one which can be applied to wines from a group of vineyards and despite its familiarity it is not especially outstanding among the other wines of Nierstein.

noble rot A mould, the scientific term for which is *Botrytis cinerea*, which affects grapes left on the vine after the normal harvest time. The condition creates a high concentration of sugar in the grapes and adds to their flavour. They then yield golden wine, ranging from sweet to lusciously sweet. The great dessert wines of Sauternes, the Rhineland, and the Tokay district of Hungary are made in this way.

In France, the term is known as *pourriture noble* and in Germany as *Edelfäule*.

non-vintage (NV) A blend; a wine that does not come from the harvest of any single year.

Norheim *(Germany)* An important, though not specially distinguished district of the Nahe region. The best of the wines come from the vineyards of Kafels, Kirschheck and Klosterberg.

North Africa A beneficent climate and French influence brought modern wines here. Red, white and rosé wine is made but, as in other warm areas, reds are nearly always the best, and very often of high alcoholic strength. Most North African wine sold in the UK is either labelled plainly under the name of its country of origin or else under a brand name. It should always be cheap. Some of the best wines are produced in Algeria, with reds that can fall not far short of the general characteristics of lesser wines from Burgundy. See **Algeria, Morocco, Tunisia**.

Nuits-Saint-Georges *(France)* Celebrated township in the Côte de Nuits, with vineyards producing fine reds and a little white. The reds are big, full-bodied and deeply flavoured. The most notable vineyard is Les Saint-Georges, the name of which was annexed by the town of Nuits nearly 100 years ago. The neighbouring village of Prémeaux is also covered by the appellation.

oeil de perdrix *(France)* Literally this means partridge eye – a term used to describe the pink tinge that can sometimes occur in white wines.

Ordinaire *(France)* The plainest variety of French wine; cheap and ordinary.

Ortenau *(Germany)* A district of the Baden region and one of the best in this area. The Riesling grape is quite widely cultivated and in a good year the wines of Ortenau can be outstanding.

Old-bottled sherry *(Spain)* Sherry that has acquired roundness and additional subtlety as a result of being kept in bottle for a period before being released on the market. The wines that respond best to this treatment are the sweeter styles. Some are matured in this way for as much as 30 years.

Oloroso *(Spain)* A sherry style, usually with considerable sweetening. Unsweetened Oloroso is full-bodied and does not possess the delicacy of the more popular Fino style.

Oppenheim *(Germany)* A major town in the Rheinhessen region with a reputation for full, round wines from its favoured south-facing vine-yards. In vintages that follow a long, warm, dry summer, Oppenheim is capable of producing finer wines than the more renowned vineyards of Nierstein.

Orvieto *(Italy)* Good white wine from vineyards around the town of Orvieto in Umbria. There are dry *(secco)* and semi-sweet *(abboccato)* versions. The dry has an attractive scent and leaves a slightly bitter taste; the semi-sweet is soft and full.

Paille, Vin de *(France)* 'Straw wine'; one that has

been pressed from grapes which have been left to dry out on straw mats. Vin de Paille is a sweet, golden wine, often strong in alcohol.

Palatinate see **Rheinpfalz**

Palo Cortado *(Spain)* An oddity among sherries, Palo Cortado is halfway between a Fino and an Oloroso. It is a wine with a magnificent aroma and nutty flavour.

Parsac *(France)* A red wine commune of the Bordeaux district of St-Émilion. It produces big wines, with little distinction, but the commune is entitled to link its name with the important St-Émilion appellation.

Passe-Tout-Grains *(France)* Red, and sometimes rosé wine made in the Burgundy region by pressing together the Pinot Noir (the great grape of red Burgundy) and the Gamay (the great grape of Beaujolais). The red version becomes better with age, and such wines made from outstanding vintages can continue to improve for a decade or more. The rosé version of this wine is for early consumption.

Passito *(Italy)* Wine, red or white, pressed from

grapes that have been allowed to dry out partially, either on the vine or after being gathered. Most are sweet, but among red wines particularly such grapes are used for blending, and the end result is often a dry, rather weighty wine.

Pauillac *(France)* A famous commune of the Bordeaux region of Haut-Médoc within the boundaries of which are some of the most celebrated châteaux, among them a greater concentration of first growths than any other commune of the Médoc. These include such château names as Latour, Lafite, Mouton-Rothschild, Pichon-Longueville, Pontet-Canet and Lynch-Bages.

The clarets of Pauillac are full-bodied, have a marked bouquet, are long lived and have great finesse. They epitomize all the best characteristics of fine claret.

Pays, Vin de *(France)* In the French *appellation contrôlée* system this is the lowest form of recognized wine. The term means, simply, 'country wine'. In fact, it embraces a reasonable handful of acceptable wines, chiefly reds, and mostly from the South of France.

Pécs *(Hungary)* District producing pleasant white wines from the Olasz Riesling grape and sound reds and rosés from the Kadarka grape.

Panadés *(Spain)* A district of Catalonia producing red, white, and rosé wines that are often above average for Spain. The best of them are red and deep-flavoured, with considerable body. Whites are less successful, but the finest of them can have considerable style. Panadés is also an important district for the production of sparkling wines, often made by the *méthode champenoise*.

perlant *(France)* Very slightly sparkling wine.

perlure d'oignon *(France)* 'Onion skin'; a term used to describe the tawny tinge acquired by some older red wines, and occasionally used to describe rosé wines.

Perlwein *(Germany)* Lightly sparkling wine, vinified purposely to give it this character.

Pessac *(France)* A distinguished commune of the Graves region and the location of some of the foremost red wine châteaux of the area, especially Haut-Brion, La Mission-Haut-Brion and Pape-Clément.

petit *(France)* Simply 'small', 'little', or in wine

parlance, 'lesser'. On a label it invariably indicates a wine that is less well regarded than the major wine of the area of district, for example Petit Chablis. Some wines so labelled can be of sound, though never outstanding, quality.

Petit Chablis *(France)* The lowest appellation in the Chablis district.

phylloxera A plant louse which attacks the vine and destroys it. In 1865 it assailed vineyards in southern France, spreading from one area to another, and from country to country. Eventually it destroyed virtually every European vineyard. A few survived because the vines were planted in sand, which discourages the louse.

Viniculture in Europe would probably have ended had it not been for the discovery that native American vine roots are resistant to phylloxera, and the remedy was found in the grafting of European vines on to American root stocks. Almost every vine in Europe today has been so treated.

Pre-phylloxera wines are sometimes offered for sale at auction; they tend to be bigger, fuller wines than those made from grapes from grafted vines.

Piedmont *(Italy)* One of Italy's most important

wine-producing provinces, with front-running wines among the reds like Barolo, Barbaresco, Barbera, Gattinara, Ghemme, Grignolino, as well as a handful of whites. It is also the area renowned for the production of Italian sparkling wines, especially in the Asti district of Piedmont, and of vermouth.

Piesport *(Germany)* A small but distinguished commune of the Mosel region, making mainly from the Riesling grape white wines of outstanding delicacy and fragrance. They are among the best of the Mosel wines. Notable vineyards include Piesporter Goldtröpfchen, Treppchen, Falkenberg and Günterslay. Wine of lesser degree may be labelled Piesporter Michelsberg or just Piesporter.

Pineau des Charentes *(France)* A sweet aperitif, made from the fermenting juice of fresh grapes in which the fermentation is halted by the addition of Cognac brandy.

Pink Champagne *(France)* Rosé Champagne, made either by allowing the skins of the black grapes to remain in contact with the grape pulp for a short time during the vintage, or else by blending red and white wines.

Pinot An important variety of black and white grape. The Pinot Noir is the classic grape of the great red Burgundy vineyards and is the main variety used in the production of Champagne. The Pinot Blanc is also an important grape in the these areas. The Pinot Gris is a less distinguished member of the same family, but is capable of producing good wine in Alsace, Italy and Germany.

All these members of the Pinot family are widely cultivated elsewhere in the wine world, but the Noir, the finest of them, is seldom as successful as it is in France.

Pinotage South African red grape variety, a cross between the Pinot Noir and the Hermitage. It produces good, warm-bodied wines.

Plonk Plain, cheap wine; an English colloquialism, thought to originate from British or Commonwealth soldiers' rendering of 'blanc' (for *vin blanc*) during the First World War. Now it is used as a derogatory term for any kind of wine, although it is not unknown for some UK wine merchants to attach it to their plainer French wines.

Pomerol *(France)* A small but important red wine district of Bordeaux, often under-rated. The wines of the district have some similarity to those of St-Émilion; they are full-bodied, fairly soft and smooth textured, but they derive an underlying distinction in flavour from the iron of the district's sub-soil, which gives them a suave, engaging taste. Another factor that plays a part in shaping the general style of clarets from this district is the widespread cultivation of the Merlot grape, which gives the wines roundness and girth. The grape also makes Pomerol wines mature fairly fast in contrast to other clarets. A Pomerol, therefore, is not a bad wine to buy when immediate drinking is called for.

District wine, labelled simply as Pomerol, is very often above the average quality of other district wines from Bordeaux, and is one of the best bets for early consumption on the retailer's shelves.

The wines of Pomerol have never been officially classified, which is perhaps just as well, since their prices would zoom up if they were to have an official accolade. But Château Pétrus is undoubtedly in the topmost rank, while other fine vineyards in the district are Château l'Évangile, Château Nénin, and Château Gazin.

Pommard *(France)* An important red wine commune of the Côte de Beaune. Its wines are famous and popular all over the world. In style they are soft, fruity, and elegant. The best vineyards include Les Épenots, Les Rugiens and Le Clos Blanc.

Port The world's most renowned fortified wine. Produced in the Alto Douro area of northern Portugal, the port trade is based chiefly in the town of Vila Nova da Gaia, on the opposite side of the River Douro from the city of Oporto. The finest style is Vintage port, made only from outstanding vintages and needing many years to mature. The basic and usually cheapest style is Ruby, aged in cask for only a few years. Tawny port may have more cask age, and therefore more refinement than Ruby, although Tawny can also be created by blending Ruby and White port, which is made only from white grapes, and may be sweet or fairly dry.

Porto, Vinho do Porto *(Portugal)* Port is the anglicized version of the wines of the Alto Douro region of Portugal. These Portuguese names sometimes appear on the labels of port bottles.

Portugal Renowned as the home of port, but also a considerable producer of light wines. Most are of an ordinary standard, but there are some important exceptions and in recent years some better-quality wines have found their way to the British market. The best known are the Vinhos Verdes of the Minho Valley; light, fresh wines with a slight sparkle, which can be red, white or rosé. The reds, however, are seldom seen outside Portugal. Good, full-bodied red wines are made in the Dão district, to the south of the port wine country. Setúbal, not far from Lisbon, produces a fine dessert wine from the Muscat grape. Finally, the island of Madeira, in the Atlantic, is a Portuguese possession famous for its fortified wines which range from lusciously sweet to moderately dry.

Pouilly-Fuissé *(France)* A good and extremely popular dry white wine of the Mâcon area. Made from the classic Chardonnay grape, it is a superbly crisp, green-gold coloured wine, fairly delicate and with an appealing nutty flavour. In recent years it has become increasingly costly, and other villages in the Mâcon area have come forward to compete with comparable wines.

Pouilly-Loché *(France)* White wine made from the Chardonnay grape in a district adjoining Pouilly-Fuissé in Mâcon. The wines are dry, crisp and fresh, and are comparable to Pouilly-Fuissé.

Pouilly-sur-Loire *(France)* Town on the banks of the Loire river. Its notable wine, a white, is Pouilly-Fumé (or Pouilly-Blanc-Fumé), a very distinctive wine made from the Sauvignon Blanc grape. It can have some sweetness in a vintage following a long, hot summer, but is generally dry and fruity. The flavour is unusual, often described as 'gunflint', the smell of steel on flint, or 'smoky'. It should be consumed while young. Lesser wines are labelled Pouilly-sur-Loire.

Pouilly-Vinzelles *(France)* A village next to Pouilly-Fuissé in Mâcon, making good dry white wines, several of which are on a par with Pouilly-Fuissé.

pourriture noble see **noble rot**

Prädikatssekt *(Germany)* The top grade of sparkling wine. Those made by the *méthode champenoise* are the best, and the producer may indicate this by using the word *Flaschengärung* (bottle fermentation) on the label.

Preignac *(France)* A sweet white wine commune of Sauternes, with the right to use the Sauternes appellation. Its best-known property is Château de Suduiraut.

Premières Côtes de Bordeaux *(France)* Appellation for red and white wines from the long, thin district of Bordeaux. White wines far outnumber reds, and are generally of a superior standard. White wine grapes include the Sémillon, Sauvignon and the Muscadelle. The wines may be dry, fairly sweet or sweet; the best of them are dry, though the sweet whites can occasionally be of high quality. Reds are made from the Cabernet and Merlot grapes, among others. They make agreeable, inexpensive wines of a modest Bordeaux style. The main commune for white wines is Cadillac.

Provence *(France)* This region has a number of wines rating as VDQS. Rosé is the front runner, in terms of output. The best of the pink wines are dry, full-flavoured and often quite powerful in alcohol. Some good reds are also made, but whites generally lack the acidity to make them acceptable on the British market. The chief districts are Bandol and Cassis.

Puisseguin-Saint-Émilion *(France)* A red wine commune of St-Émilion with the right to share the appellation. The wines are full-bodied and sound, and represent good value among secondary clarets.

Puligny-Montrachet *(France)* Commune in the Côte de Beaune with a high reputation for fine dry white wines. About half of the area of the greatest vineyard sites, Le Montrachet and Bâtard-Montrachet, lie in the neighbouring commune of Chassagne-Montrachet, but Puligny, like Chassagne, has fine vineyard sites of its own, including Chevalier-Montrachet, Bienvenues-Bâtard-Montrachet and Les Combettes. Wine from these exalted vineyards is never inexpensive, but some of the lesser wines of the commune are of a very high standard and at more comfortable prices.

punt The inward bulge at the base of a bottle, especially of Champagne. Its purpose is not to deprive the customer of a small quantity of wine, but to strengthen the bottle. All sparkling wines require a strong bottle since the pressure within is considerable.

puttony *(Hungary)* A tub in which grapes are collected. In Tokay the *puttony* is a measure of the richness of fine sweet wines. Each *puttony* of *aszú* (sweet, late-gathered, specially selected grapes) added before fermentation to the normal must gives the wine its grade. Usually there are four such grades: three, four, five and six *puttonyos* (or *putts*, as the plural of the word is abbreviated). Six *puttonyos* Tokay is, however, a rarity. Prices rise according to the ascending order of the grade. The number of *puttonyos* is shown on the neck label.

Qualitätswein *(Germany)* A grade of wine, under German wine laws, that is above *Tafelwein*. Frequently abbreviated to QW or QbA, it is recognized by the authorities as a wine originating from a defined area. Such wines will be reasonably full-bodied and will typify the general style of wines of their district of origin.

Qualitätswein bestimmter Anbaugebiet *(Germany)* Often shortened to QbA, this denotes, under German wine law, a quality wine from any one of Germany's eleven officially recognized wine-producing regions. Such wines must reach a specified alcoholic strength, show the general characteristics of the wine of the region, and obtain official approval of quality. Their labels may also declare the district (Bereich) within the region, the group of vineyards (Grosslage) and the individual vineyard (Einzellage).

Qualitätswein mit Prädikat *(Germany)* Usually shortened to QmP. This is the finest category of German wines, in which there are five grades.

These, in ascending order, are Kabinett, Spätlese, Auslese, Beerenauslese and Trockenbeerenauslese. Eiswein is a projection of the latter grade.

Quarts de Chaume *(France)* A famous vineyard of the Coteaux du Layon in the Loire region. Its wine, made from the Chenin grape, is sweet and luscious, smooth-textured and golden coloured. It has been compared with the better growths of Sauternes, and it commands a high price.

Quincy *(France)* A village of the Loire region giving its name to attractive, light-bodied white wines made from the Sauvignon grape.

quinta *(Portugal)* An estate, vineyard, or the buildings attached thereto. Some port wine producers market wine under the name of their best *quinta*, rather than (but sometimes as well as) the more common practice of using the proprietorial name.

Rainwater *(Portugal)* Originally a brand name for a blend of Madeira, Rainwater has become a generally used term for a pale, light version of Madeira, either dry or medium sweet.

Randersacker *(Germany)* An important centre in

Franconia producing wines of a quality that can compare with the region's most notable, from Würzburg. Leading vineyard names include Teufelskeller and Pfülben.

Ratafia Traditionally, this was a drink that was taken as a toast upon the ratification of a treaty or agreement, but now it is seldom heard of in diplomatic circles. Ratafia is a fortified wine, made by halting the fermentation of grape juice by the addition of spirit. It has similarities to Pineau des Charentes with the same heavy, rather musty taste; sometimes it is flavoured with herbs, fruits and spices.

Ratafia is now rarely available, but major wine merchants in the UK may stock Ratafia de Champagne or Ratafia de Bourgogne. It can be taken as an aperitif, well chilled.

Rauenthal *(Germany)* A small village in the Rheingau region. Its wines are rated among the region's finest, and they are regularly among the most costly. They have an intense bouquet and a very attractive spiciness in their flavour. Among the best vineyards are Baiken, Gehrn, Langenstück and Rothenberg.

Recioto *(Italy)* White or red wine made from

specially selected over-ripe grapes which are allowed partially to dry out. It is a popular wine in the Valpolicella area near Verona. Most versions of it are sweet, but a dry style, Amarone, is also produced.

récolte *(France)* The harvest. The word is sometimes used in conjunction with the vintage date on labels.

Retsina *(Greece)* Red or rosé light wine that has been treated with pine resin. This is done during the period of fermentation, when pieces of pine resin, traditionally from Attica, are added to the grape juice. The process of resinating wine originated in ancient Greece when a mixture of plaster and resin was used to seal amphoras; the resin affected the flavour of the wine and this taste found favour. Retsina, reminiscent of wine that has been in contact with turpentine, is an acquired taste.

Reuilly *(France)* A minor district of the Loire. It makes an agreeable dry white wine from the Sauvignon grape.

Rheims, Reims *(France)* Principal centre of the Champagne region, and home of the majority of

Champagne producers. They include Heidsieck Monopole, Charles Heidsieck, Lanson, Krug, Pommery and Greno, Louis Roederer, Taittinger and Veuve Clicquot-Ponsardin.

Rhein *(Germany)* The German spelling of Rhine.

Rheingau *(Germany)* One of the eleven designated German wine regions, and the producer of some of the finest Rhine wines, all of which are white. The quality of the wine is influenced decisively by the lie of the land, which is almost all south-facing and overlooking the Rhine river, so that the vineyards absorb not only direct sunlight but reflected sunlight from the river. More than three-quarters of the total area are planted with the Riesling grape, which in this region attains its peak of perfection.

The overall character of wines from the Rheingau region is fruity and elegant, with a lingering after-taste, and they have an intense bouquet. The best are long-lasting. World-famous villages within the region include Erbach, Hattenheim, Johannisberg, Rüdesheim, Hochheim, Rauenthal, Hallgarten and Winkel. Some red wine is also produced for which there is a steady demand within Germany. But it is for its great Riesling wines that the region is justly renowned.

Rheinhessen *(Germany)* One of the eleven officially designated wine-growing regions of the Federal Republic. The finest wines are made from the Riesling grape, but only about four or five per cent of plantings in the region are of this variety, the main one being of the less distinguished vine, the Müller-Thurgau.

Rheinhessen is the principal producer of one of the plainer styles of German wine, Liebfraumilch, and the city of Worms is the location of the Liebfrauenstift vineyards, where the original Liebfraumilch was made. Today the designation has a far wider application. The original vineyards at Liebfrauenstift are still productive though the wine they produce has no particular merit, better wines being made elsewhere, especially in Nierstein, Oppenheim, Nackenheim, Bingen and Dienheim.

Rheinpfalz *(Germany)* Alternatively known as the Palatinate, this is the second largest of the eleven officially designated wine-producing regions of the Federal Republic of Germany. The principal grape is the Müller-Thurgau, which occupies about a quarter of the region's vine plantings, followed by the Sylvaner, with about 18 per cent and by the Riesling with about $13\frac{1}{2}$ per cent. The region is named after the Palatine Hill in

Rome, where the emperors' palaces were built, and this distinction doubtless resulted from the long period in which the region was known as 'the Holy Roman Empire's wine-cellar', and palace officials, including those who had charge of the cellar, were 'Palatinate' men.

A wide range of wines is produced, appealing especially to those with a taste for firm, full-bodied wine. Outstanding years in the Rheinpfalz can produce wines that are almost as full as those of the more widely famed Rheingau region, strong and hearty. The best districts are Wachenheim, Deidesheim, Bad Dürkheim, Forst and Ruppertsberg.

Rhône *(France)* A major region producing red, white, rosé and sparkling wines in a wide variety of styles. It is best known for its big-bodied reds, often of high alcoholic strength and long-lived. The whites and rosés are also usually full-flavoured. Main districts of the Rhône are Châteauneuf-du-Pape, Côte Rôtie, Condrieu, Cornas, Crozes-Hermitage, Gigondas, Hermitage, Saint-Joseph, Saint-Péray, Tavel, and Lirac. Côtes du Rhône is the appellation for lesser wines of the Rhône valley.

Rice wine see **Saké**

Riesling One of the world's most widely cultivated white wine grapes, with a number of sub-
varieties. Its finest wines are made in Germany
from the original Rhine-Riesling, and they range
from dry to lusciously sweet. The grape also
produces outstanding wine in Alsace. Other varieties are Olasz, Italico and Welschriesling (or
Walschriesling). All can produce good, acceptable
wines but never as distinguished as the original
Riesling in its home territory.

Rioja *(Spain)* Red and white wines are made
here, in Spain's smallest wine-growing area,
where some of the best wines on the Iberian
Peninsula are produced. The region escaped the
phylloxera blight and was settled by French
growers who imported many of their skills to the
area. Rioja is more suited to the production of red
wine than of white. Comparable whites can be
found in other wine-producing areas of Europe
and are not particularly important but Rioja reds
are among the better wines of Europe, and will be
modestly priced alongside those of similar quality
from France and even Italy. They have a powerful
body and remarkable suppleness.

Owing to the traditions of Rioja they can be
held in cask for many years and thus acquire a
'woody' flavour that is not altogether agreeable to

the British taste for 'clean' wines. Nonetheless, Rioja reds selected for the British market are, in general, good, solid wines for drinking with steaks or casseroles.

The centre of the Rioja wine industry is Haro, and another name to appear on labels is Fuenmayor. Under Spanish wine laws the Rioja area has been delineated and fakes on the UK market are unlikely, though the official seal does not carry with it a guarantee of quality. District names are not, so far, important, since most red Rioja is sold under the producers' names. Reserva is a wine that has been kept for some time in wood and Reserva Especial will be an older wine.

Rödelsee *(Germany)* A good district in the region of Franconia. Among the best vineyards are Küchenmeister and Hoheleite.

rosato *(Italy)* The Italian name for rosé or pink wine.

rosso *(Italy)* The Italian for red wine.

Roussillon see **Languedoc-Roussillon**

Roxheim *(Germany)* A good district in the designated Nahe wine-producing region.

Rubesco Torgiano see **Torgiano**

Ruby port The plainest, and usually the cheapest, style of port, kept in cask for about five or six years before being marketed. These ports are not designed to improve in bottle and are less refined than Tawny.

Rüdesheim *(Germany)* A town of the Nahe region. Rosengarten is the best known vineyard in the locality. In exceptional years the wines of Rüdesheim can have considerable style, but they are not of particular distinction.

There are two wine-producing districts of this name. The other, in the Rheingau region, is the better.

Rüdesheim *(Germany)* A small town in the Rheingau region with steep, sun-exposed vineyards which have a reputation for producing above-average wines even in years that are poor or indifferent in other districts of the Rheingau. Because of the lie of the vineyards, however, a hot, dry summer can make wine that is untypically heavy and of uneven balance.

The best vineyards are those of Rüdesheimerberg, making in an average year relatively light, fruity wines which can show much style.

Ruländer *(Germany)* The name by which the Pinot Gris grape is known in Germany.

Rully *(France)* White wines from this commune of the Côte Chalonnaise are becoming better known. They are dry and fresh, and can have considerable fruitiness. The commune has been long established as an important centre for the production of sparkling Burgundy.

Romania One of the top ten in terms of output among the world's wine-producing countries. Sound red wines are made from several of the classic grape varieties of Western Europe, such as the Cabernet, Pinot Noir and Merlot. Many of the white wines are medium sweet or sweet. Classic grapes used in the production of whites include the Chardonnay, Traminer, Riesling and Furmint and a profusion of Balkan grape varieties.

A wine which is a speciality is Cotnari, a luscious natural dessert wine with some similarity to Tokay, though without the same great concentration of flavour. Wine production in Romania has been extensively modernized and standards are advancing rapidly. Although little known on the British market, there is every prospect that Romanian wines will become steadily more important here.

Ruppertsberg *(Germany)* A district in the Rheinpfalz region. It has a high reputation for the pronounced, even remarkable, fruitiness of its wines. Distinguished vineyard names include Hoheburg, Gaisböhl and Nussbien.

Ruwer *(Germany)* A tributary of the Mosel river. See **Mosel-Saar-Ruwer**.

Saar *(Germany)* A tributary of the Mosel river. See **Mosel-Saar-Ruwer**.

Saint-Amour *(France)* Most northerly of the important communes in the red wine area of Beaujolais. It makes a light, almost delicate wine with a lot of fruit and a delectable bouquet. A wine of great charm, it is for early drinking.

Saint-Chinian *(France)* A red, white and rosé wine district of the Languedoc-Roussillon·area. Most of the wine produced is light, fairly soft red of acceptable quality.

Sainte-Croix-du-Mont *(France)* A small district of Bordeaux, not far from Sauternes, using the same grape varieties and methods and capable of producing in a good year golden, full-bodied sweet wines akin to those of Sauternes, but never attaining the breeding and finesse of the better Sauternes wines.

Saint-Émilion *(France)* A distinguished red wine of Bordeaux. The vineyards make some of the finest clarets, full-bodied and rich, which have sometimes been compared with the better red wines of Burgundy. St-Émilion wines, however, have a distinctive character of their own, the best of them having immense fruitiness and a fine, soft, velvet texture in the mouth. Wines from a good vintage will need at least eight years to attain complete maturity, and sometimes, in an exceptional year, more. The Merlot grape, yielding soft, easy-to-drink wine, is the predominant variety, giving St-Émilion clarets their distinctive character.

The centre of the district is the town of St-Émilion, and in its environs most of the better vineyards are located, but a number of other communes have the right to the St-Émilion appellation, and are entitled to attach the name to their own.

St-Émilion wines were classified in 1955, with two outstanding vineyards, Château Ausone and Château Cheval-Blanc, at the head of a list of 'first great growths'. Also among the twelve are Château Figeac, Château Bel-Air, Château Canon, and Château Pavie, and others are of comparable merit. There is a second 'league' of wines totalling about 70 vineyards classed as 'great growths'.

As elsewhere in Bordeaux, much of the wine is sold simply under the district name. Plain St-Émilion has none of the depth or classic style of the wines of the finer properties of the district, but normally they manage to reflect the general style of the clarets from this area and a plain, relatively inexpensive 'St-Émilion' is certainly likely to be one of the best buys among generic clarets. Localities with a special claim to fame include St-Georges, Montagne, Lussac and Puisseguin.

Saint-Estèphe *(France)* Most northerly of the four famous communes of the Haut-Médoc, Bordeaux. It borders the lesser area of Bas-Médoc and some of its wines bearing the plain St-Estèphe appellation can be of below-average quality for the Haut-Médoc. St-Estèphe produces some of the driest clarets, big-bodied and generally very fruity and with a pronounced bouquet. There are no first growths within the commune, but two notable second-growth châteaux are Montrose and Cos d'Estournel, and a distinguished third growth is Château Calon-Ségur.

Saint-Georges-Saint-Émilion *(France)* A commune of St-Émilion producing sound red wines which are entitled to share the St-Émilion appellation.

Saint-Joseph *(France)* A red and white wine district of the Rhône valley. The reds have more delicacy than is common among Rhône reds, with a less assertive body than the majority. The whites are acceptable but rather lighter than typical Rhône whites.

Sainte-Foy-Bordeaux *(France)* Bordeaux appellation for sweet white wines, some made by the Sauternes method in which grapes are left late on the vine to achieve a high sugar concentration. Small quantities of red are also made.

Saint-Julien *(France)* One of the four most celebrated communes of the Haut-Médoc in Bordeaux. The district is considered to produce a style of claret that is particularly acceptable to the British palate, with a fragrant bouquet, a big concentration of fruit and a very full flavour, and the wine is relatively speedy to mature.

St-Julien lies in the very heart of the Haut-Médoc, and even though it has no first growths, its location enables it to produce a great many wines of distinction. Even the plain appellation of the commune name indicates a wine of sound quality. Of the five second-growth châteaux in St-Julien, three are prefixed Léoville (Las Cases, Poyferré and Barton). The two others are Château Gruaud-Larose and Château Ducru-Beaucaillou.

Saint Macaire *(France)* Southern zone of the Côtes de Bordeaux, producing sweet white wines of reasonable quality, and some dry whites.

Saint-Péray *(France)* A village of the Rhône region. Much of the production is of sparkling white wines made by the *méthode champenoise*. They are of excellent quality and are among the best sparkling wines of France outside Champagne, with a full body. The still dry white wines are sound but not outstanding.

Saint-Raphaël *(France)* A proprietary wine-based aperitif, flavoured with quinine and herbs.

Saint-Véran *(France)* Dry white wine from a district adjoining Pouilly-Fuissé in the Mâcon area. The wines are made from the Chardonnay grape, as is Pouilly-Fuissé, and are akin in character to the wines of the more famous neighbour.

Saké *(Japan)* A colourless liquor made in Japan, which can be categorized as half-way between wine and beer. It is quite sweet, and in Japan it is traditionally served warm.

Salvagnin *(Switzerland)* Generic name for the red wines of Vaud.

Samos *(Greece)* Aegean island making one of the few Greek wines of renown, a sweet white dessert wine with the pronounced perfume of the Muscat grape from which it is made. The island also produces dry wines but they are of no special distinction.

Sancerre *(France)* A district of the Loire. Red, white and rosé wines are made and though the reds are of no special merit, the whites, made from the Sauvignon Blanc grape, are good pale dry wines with a trace of flint. The rosés of Sancerre are made from the Pinot Noir grape; they are dry and firm and rated as one of the few serious pink wines made anywhere. Both the red and the rosé need to be consumed when they are still young.

Santa Maddalena *(Italy)* Fresh, fruity, light red wine from the Trentino-Alto Adige region.

Santenay *(France)* A village in the south of the

Côte de Beaune. Some white wines are made, but the reds are better. They are on the light side for Burgundy, and quick to mature, but can be exceptionally fruity. These wines are often relatively inexpensive, and can represent very good value for money.

Santo, Vino *(Italy)* A speciality of the region of Tuscany, but also produced elsewhere in Italy. The wine is made from grapes that have been allowed to dry out to some extent. It has a fine, golden colour and is a wine of considerable sweetness.

Sardinia *(Italy)* A substantial producer of plain wine; one of the more interesting, Vernaccia, takes its name from the grape variety from which it is made.

Saumur *(France)* An extensive area of the province of Anjou, producing red, white and rosé wines along the south bank of the Loire river. Most of the wine output of Saumur is white and rather sharp, but it can attain some suppleness if it is given bottle age. In the UK the most frequently encountered style is also white, but has been transformed into a sparkling wine, which is crisp, light and dry and makes a good aperitif.

Sauternes *(France)* One of five communes with the right to the appellation Sauternes and which between them produce one of the world's finest sweet white wines. The others are Barsac, which is entitled to use its own appellation as well as that of Sauternes, Bommes, Fargues, and Preignac. The most renowned property is Château d'Yquem, which was exclusively classified as the 'first great growth' in the classification of 1855. It is followed in the classification by eleven first growths and twelve second growths, more than the number appearing in the original classification because some properties have been divided over the years. There are many other properties in the five communes. Cheap Sauternes will not have the rich, honeyed sweetness for which the wines of the area are famous.

The main grape is the Sémillon, which is harvested late when half-rotten and so with a considerable concentration of sugar. The wines mature five or six years after the vintage. Production is labour-intensive and the yields are not large, so that good Sauternes will always be costly, especially the produce of Château d'Yquem. First and second growths, however, can often offer good value.

Sauvignon Blanc A white wine grape and the

source of many of the world's finest white wines. Its most distinguished results are in the Bordeaux region where, blended with wine from other grapes, it is the backbone of wines ranging from dry Graves to the finest growths of Sauternes. Elsewhere in France it is among the noble varieties for white wines made in Burgundy and is also prominent in the Loire Valley, where it is known as the Blanc Fumé. The grape also has good results in the Americas, notably in California and in Chile.

Savennières *(France)* Small village in the Anjou-Coteaux de la Loire. Its robust dry white wines, made from the Chenin grape, are the best of the area.

Savigny-les-Beaune *(France)* A major red and white wine commune of the Côte de Beaune. Its reds are fairly light for Burgundy, but they have an appealing fruity suppleness. They are quick to mature. The whites are good sound dry wines. The commune has no wines of great renown, but its products are reliable and usually moderately priced. The notable vineyard is Vergelesses.

Savoie, Haute Savoie *(France)* Best known in the UK for good sparkling wines, but it is also a producer of extremely light-coloured and light-flavoured still dry wines, and a little red. The two best districts are Seyssel and Crépy.

Schaumwein *(Germany)* A term for sparkling wine. Although it may be applied to any kind of sparkling wine, it normally indicates wine of the lowest category. *Qualitätschaumwein* is of a higher standard.

Scheurebe A white wine grape variety, a comparatively recent hybrid obtained by crossing the Riesling and the Sylvaner. The grape makes big-bodied, aromatic wines.

Schloss Böckelheim *(Germany)* One of the outstanding districts of the Nahe region. Its greatest vineyard site is the Kupfergrube, a hill which was a copper mine before vines were planted on its sunny slope. Another vineyard of distinction is Felsenberg.

sediment Particles or dregs formed from grapes. Such a deposit does not imply any fault in the wine. It is usually found in good quality reds and in some fortified wines, including better qualities of port. Careful pouring can ensure that sediment remains in the bottle.

Sekt *(Germany)* A German word for sparkling wines. The best are made in the Rhine and Mosel-Saar-Ruwer regions and will be made from wine produced from grapes that come solely from the region of origin. Others are a mixture of German and imported grapes, but must contain a minimum of 60 per cent German grapes.

Sémillon A white grape variety of distinction. In the Sauternes district of Bordeaux it is the grape which, left on the vine until well after normal harvesting time, is affected by the 'noble rot', resulting in a substantial concentration of sugar. It is therefore the principal source of the great sweet white wines of Sauternes. The Sémillon is also cultivated elsewhere in France, and in California and Australia, but outside France it never gives the fine wine.

Sercial *(Portugal)* The driest style of Madeira, not unlike dry sherry but with considerably more weight. It is an aperitif wine.

Setúbal *(Portugal)* An exceedingly good dessert wine made near Lisbon from the Muscat grape. It has a fine bouquet and a large flavour. Setúbal is made on the same principle as port, with the fermentation being ended by the addition of brandy. The older wines – unlikely to be obtained outside Portugal – can attain great finesse.

Sèvre-et-Maine *(France)* Section of the Loire Valley producing Muscadet of notable quality.

Seyssel *(France)* A district of Savoie producing pale, extremely dry white wine. Much of it is made into sparkling wine, which is regarded as one of the best sparklers made outside the Champagne region.

Sherry *(Spain)* Fortified wine produced in Andalucia, southern Spain, although versions of 'sherry' are made in many other countries. All sherries are blends, using the solera system in which older wines are mixed with the newer, enabling producers of a brand to ensure its consistency of taste over the years. The main styles of sherry are Fino, Manzanilla, Amontillado, Oloroso and Cream, though there are several sub-styles such as Golden, Palo Cortado, Amoroso and Brown. See also **South Africa, Cyprus**.

Sicily *(Italy)* Large Mediterranean island, most notable for the production of a fortified wine, Marsala. Among light wines, the majority are of a rather ordinary standard, with a tendency to retain some of the 'burnt' flavour of the volcanic soil. One of the better vineyard areas near Palermo produces good white and red wines (but mostly white) under the name of Corvo di Casteldaccia.

Sizzano see **Ghemme**

Soave *(Italy)* Very good dry, pale white wine made in a zone surrounding the village of Soave to the north of Verona. It is light in body, has a good flowery bouquet, and is intended for drinking within three years of the vintage, otherwise it will lose its freshness. Soave is considered to be the best of the dry Italian white wines.

solera *(Spain)* The blending system used by sherry producers. The solera is a tier of casks containing wines of differing ages, with the youngest wine on the top tier, the oldest on the lowest. As wine is drawn off from the bottom tier, it is replenished from the next oldest, on the tier above. This is in turn replenished with wine on the next tier up, and the process continues until all the casks, except those containing the oldest wine, have given some of their contents to those below them. The system enables a producer to maintain the quality and character of his wine over the years.

Sopron *(Hungary)* A district near the Austrian border, best known for agreeable, lively red wines made from the Kékfrankos grape (Soproni Kékfrankos).

South Africa An important producer of almost every style of wine, many of very high quality. The best vineyards are within a short distance of Cape Town, in the Paarl valley and the district of Stellenbosch. Excellent dry white wines are made from the Riesling and the Steen, a local grape variety; late-harvested Steen grapes also make a fruity medium-dry wine. Notable reds include Pinotage, a full wine pressed from a grape variety that is a cross between the Hermitage and Pinot Noir, and other good reds made from the Cabernet Sauvignon, Cinsault, and Gamay.

Production of fortified wine is extensive; the better Tawny and Ruby port styles can be remarkably distinguished. But the most familiar fortified wine from South Africa on the UK market is sherry style. The vineyards lie on nearly the same latitude as the original sherry vineyards of Spain, and the winemakers faithfully follow the original Spanish production system. The results are of very high standard, and the sweet and medium sweet versions of South African sherry can be indistinguishable from the Spanish product. Good dry sherry-style wines are also made, but the best of them do not compare with the best Spanish Finos.

South America see **Argentina, Chile**

Spain Famous for sherry and well known as a producer of inexpensive light wines of a rather plain kind, but now also an increasingly important source of quality light wines at comparatively moderate prices. Although Spain has a greater acreage of land under vines than France, her output is only about one-third of French output. This low yield is partly accounted for by the arid climate, partly by the continuing use of rudimentary methods on a fairly widespread scale. There are important exceptions to this, including Andalucia, where sherry is produced, and Rioja, a district of Aragon, where methods have been influenced by French tradition.

Spanna *(Italy)* Name used in the Piedmont region for the noble Nebbiolo grape.

Spätburgunder *(Germany)* The German equivalent of the Pinot Noir, a distinguished grape variety.

Spätlese *(Germany)* A wine made from late-gathered grapes. The grapes reach a more advanced state of maturity than those gathered at the normal harvest time, and therefore have a richer sugar content. Spätlese wines tend to be fuller in body and a shade sweeter than the general run of German white wines. See also **Auslese, Beerenauslese, Trockenbeerenauslese**.

Spritzig *(Germany)* Very slightly sparkling wine.

Spumante *(Italy)* The Italian name for sparkling wine. The most highly regarded of Italian sparkling wines come from the Asti district, near Turin. Spumante wines are made extensively elsewhere in Italy, but only Asti is significant on the UK market.

Still Champagne *(France)* White wine produced in the Champagne area which does not go through the Champagne process, and therefore does not sparkle. Some red is also made. The appellation for both these still wines is Coteaux Champenois.

still wine A wine, other than fortified wine, which has not been made to sparkle. Some, however, may have a slight prickle on the tongue, or petillance, which is induced by the maker (especially in Italy). Nevertheless, these still count as still wines.

Styria *(Austria)* A region in Austria. The vineyards, planted with an extensive variety of vines, produce white and red wines, of which the whites are sound, usually dry and flowery.

Superiore *(Italy)* On Italian labels, this is an indication that the wine is of the highest grade of its district.

sur lie *(France)* Wine that is bottled along with its lees, or sediment. Normally this deposit is left behind in the casks, but deliberate bottling of a wine along with some of its lees is practised in some areas, particularly in the Loire region among wines made from the Muscadet grape. The resulting wine is more strongly flavoured than wines that have been filtered off the lees, but it needs to be carefully decanted.

Switzerland A country producing an extensive variety of light wines, chiefly white. Swiss growers have a high degree of skill, and the wines are generally extremely well made. Some are interesting, but none is of outstanding merit. White wine, which constitutes the bulk of Swiss production, is light and often thin; some of it is *pétillant*. Mostly it is made from the Chasellas grape, known in Switzerland as the Fendant, which is little rated elsewhere but is especially well suited to cool regions. The Sylvaner, renamed the Johannisberger in Switzerland, is also grown, and makes a wine that is generally more agreeable than the Fendant.

The better wines are made in French Switzerland, notably Vaud, Neuchâtel and the Valais, but the Italian-speaking canton of Ticino produces some acceptable reds made from the Merlot grape.

Sylvaner, Silvaner A white wine grape variety, widely cultivated in Germany and in the Alsace region of France. It produces a light, refreshing wine, for quaffing. In Germany, if left on the vine, it is capable of making rich, sweet wines.

Syrah A red wine grape, especially distinguished for its role in the production of Hermitage. The wine it makes is big, powerful and slow to mature. It has been successfully cultivated in

California, South Africa and elsewhere, but does not perform as successfully outside the Rhône Valley as it does within it.

Tafelwein *(Germany)* Simply, this means table wine. It is the lowest grade in the German wine hierarchy, a blend which may contain wines from other EEC countries.

Talence *(France)* An important commune of Graves producing red and white wines. Leading properties include Château La Tour-Haut-Brion for red wine and Château Laville-Haut-Brion, the source of one of the most distinguished of white Graves.

Tarragona *(Spain)* Wine region of Spain, and a large producer of ordinary red and white table wine, much of which is used in blending. It is also the source of sweet, red fortified wine, marketed in Britain as Tarragona.

Tavel *(France)* A village of the Rhône region famous for one of the finest rosés produced anywhere. It is a dry wine with a vigorous body, good bouquet and strong in alcohol. As with other rosés, it is best consumed while young and still fresh.

Tawny port An elegant style of port which spends many years in cask becoming lighter in body and in colour. True Tawny port produced in this way is always expensive. A cheaper, far less meritorious style is made by blending young Ruby port with White port.

Tête de Cuvée *(France)* Implicitly, the best; the words indicate that the wine in the bottle has been made from the first, and therefore the finest, pressing of the grapes. It is most usually encountered among Champagnes.

Ticino An Italian-speaking canton of Switzerland which in the last couple of decades has considerably improved the quality of its red wines, chiefly by introducing the French Merlot grape. Ticino Merlots are agreeable, soft wines with a good bouquet but little backbone.

Tokay *(Hungary)* Premier wine-producing region, and probably the most famous in Europe outside France and Germany. Several styles of wine are made, but the finest one, with world-wide renown, is a fine white dessert wine. Distinctive, but less exceptional wines bearing the Tokay appellation are Szamorodni and Furmint. But it is for its sweet dessert wines that Tokay has its high reputation. They are pressed from the Furmint, Hárslevelü and yellow Muscat grapes, left to ripen and over-ripen on the vines in the mellow autumn season of the region. In these conditions they become susceptible to the 'noble rot'; they shrivel and become heavily concentrated with natural sugar. These grapes are known as *Aszu*, and the wine that is pressed from them has immense body and richness. The degree of richness is measured in *puttonyos*, shown on the label as 'putts'. The more there are, the richer the wine will be.

Tokay d'Alsace *(France)* The name by which the Pinot Gris grape is known in Alsace, where it makes a dry, earthy white wine. It has nothing to do with the great sweet wines of Tokay in Hungary.

Tokay Furmint *(Hungary)* A wine produced from Furmint grapes in the Tokay district of Hungary. It has no special distinction above that of many of the wines produced from the same grape elsewhere in Hungary.

Tokay Szamorodni *(Hungary)* A style of Tokay, sometimes sweet or semi-sweet, depending on the volume of late-gathered, over-ripe grapes that goes into its production, but dry when the wine is made from grapes ripened in the ordinary way. Tokay Szamorodni is a wine of lesser distinction than Aszu. The label should indicate whether the wine is dry or semi-sweet.

Torgiano *(Italy)* A high-quality red wine comparable with a good full claret. Torgiano is a small district in Umbria, which also produces some white wine. The red is called Rubesco Torgiano.

Toscano *(Italy)* Wine from Tuscany. On labels in Britain the words usually suggest a carafe wine of above-average quality.

Touraine *(France)* One of the largest districts of the Loire. Red, white, rosé and sparkling wines are made, of which the best known is the white Vouvray, in both its still and sparkling versions. Montlouis is the source of white wines of a similar style. Bourgueil and Chinon have a sound reputation for their full-bodied reds.

Tours-sur-Marne *(France)* Centre of the Champagne region, and headquarters of the House of Laurent-Perrier.

Traminer A white grape variety, making soft,

spicy wine, especially characteristic of Alsace.

transfer system A method of producing sparkling wine. The wine is fermented and matured in bottle, as in the *méthode champenoise*, but is then disgorged into tanks. The sediment sinks and the wine can then be bottled.

Trentino–Alto Adige *(Italy)* Northern area of Italy, producing chiefly white wines in the German or Austrian style, but also some reds. Most are labelled with the name of the grape variety, for example Riesling, Sylvaner and Traminer. There are also some grape varieties peculiar to the region. In general, the whites are acceptable though not distinguished.

trocken *(Germany)* Literally, this means dry. Thoroughly dry Rhine and Moselle wines were, until recently, primarily for domestic consumption, since overseas markets, including the UK, preferred styles with some degree of sweetness. Lately they have become increasingly popular in Germany's major overseas markets.

Trockenbeerenauslese *(Germany)* One of the finest of the sweet white wines of Germany, more rare and concentrated even than Beerenauslese. It is pressed from grapes that are left so late on the vine that they become sun-shrivelled, and are affected by 'noble rot'. Wines made from these grapes are among the richest in the world, with a superb depth of flavour and aroma; their richness is reflected in their high price.

Tunisia *(North Africa)* A former French protectorate and source of decent-quality light wine, mostly red, selling inexpensively, and more or less anonymously, in the UK. Although vines have been cultivated in Tunisia for many hundreds of years, the basis of the modern wine industry was established by French settlers, and is therefore relatively sophisticated. The reds are usually fairly high in alcohol.

Tunisian wines are generally sold under a brand name in Britain and although certain areas of the country can produce wines of distinctly good quality, placenames are not of any consequence.

Tuscany *(Italy)* One of the most famous of the wine regions of Italy. It includes the Chianti area, producer of Italy's best-known red wine, which accounts for about a quarter of Tuscany's total wine output.

But much of the region's red and white wine is sold under the main heading Toscana, or Toscano. These are plain light wines, red or white, and are usually good value.

Umbria *(Italy)* A central province, one of the smallest in Italy, with one renowned wine, Orvieto, that has a place in the world's wine charts. But a good red is produced in the small area of Torgiano.

United States of America No fewer than 28 states produce wine, but California is by far the largest contributor and the only state to make quality wines in volume from European wine stocks. Native American vines and some hybrids are cultivated in several eastern states with New York State as the chief producer, but these wines are seldom encountered outside the US.

Valais *(Switzerland)* A canton of French Switzerland. Red wines made from the Gamay and Pinot Noir grape varieties are known as Dôle. Agreeable soft, light, dry whites are made from the Chasselas grape, known in Switzerland as the Fendant, and pleasant Riesling-style wines are made from the Johannisberger grape, as the Sylvaner is called there.

Valpolicella *(Italy)* A popular red wine made in

the vicinity of the village of Valpolicella in the Veneto region. Most of it is light, refreshing, and fragrant, to be consumed within a year or so of the vintage. Another style, Valpolicella Superiore, is aged for longer in cask and takes on more weight, but it is not a long-lived wine.

varietals General term for wines that are sold mainly under the name of the grape from which they have been pressed, rather than under district, regional or brand names. The practice has been long established in Alsace, for example Gewürz-traminer, Riesling and Sylvaner, in eastern and central Europe (particularly for Rieslings), and in California.

The marketing of wines under their own variet-al names is now increasing, and the British market has seen the introduction of Bulgarian Pinot Chardonnay, Yugoslavian Cabernet Sauvignon, and so on. The trend is a good one for the consumer; such names at least indicate the general style of wine to be expected.

Vaud *(Switzerland)* A canton of French Switzer-land, notable for light-bodied white wines made from the Chasselas grape, which is known there as the Fendant. The generic name for Vaud whites is Dorin.

VDQS see **Appellation d'Origine Contrôlée**

Veneto *(Italy)* A name that covers the whole of the area in the region of Venice. Many of Italy's most renowned wines are produced here, including Bardolino, Valpolicella and Soave. But other, lesser wines are also made in the area.

Verdelho *(Portugal)* A medium sweet style of Madeira wine with a dry after-taste.

Verdicchio *(Italy)* Grape variety grown with good results in the Marche region of Italy. The wine is characterized by its dry, clean flavour and freshness. Verdicchio dei Castelli di Jesi is one of the best.

Vergini *(Italy)* The driest style of Marsala but not, on account of its full flavour and rather hearty character, a leader among the aperitif wines.

vermouth A wine-based aperitif, about the same strength as sherry, which was once used almost exclusively as an ingredient of cocktails but has in the last two decades or so been taken as a drink either without any additive or else with soda. The wines that form the basis of vermouth are generally of indifferent quality, and are flavoured with herbs, spices, seeds and bark. The main flavouring agent is wormwood, and it is from the German rendering of this shrub, *Wermut*, that the drink takes its name.

Traditionally, France was the centre for light, dry vermouths while Italy was noted for its heavier, dark sweet versions. Now each country makes both styles. Comparatively new creations are sweet white Vermouth Bianco and a drier rosé style. Besides these two traditional centres vermouth is made in various other countries.

Vernacchia *(Italy)* A white wine from Sardinia made from the grape of the same name. Strongly flavoured, it could take the place of a red wine to accompany robust Italian dishes.

vignoble *(France)* A vineyard area; a group of vineyards having a shared appellation.

Vin, Vino, Vinho The general terms for wine in, respectively, France, Spain and Italy, and Portugal. For specialized wine terms, see entries under these words or under the word that qualifies them, for example, Corriente, Gris, Jaune and Paille.

Vin de l'Année *(France)* Literally, 'this year's

wine'. The term covers any wine from the end of one vintage until the start of the next.

Vinho Verde *(Portugal)* The 'green' (barely ripened) light wines of northern Portugal can be white, red or rosé but it is the whites that are best known and most appreciated. They are low in alcohol, sharp on the palate, and usually have a slight sparkle. Vinho Verde wines designated for export markets are often sweetened, which causes them to lose some of their crisp freshness.

vinification The making of wine; the process by which wine is produced.

vintage The grape harvest. In Europe vintaging takes place from about September, but in certain parts of France and Germany it can run on for some weeks later. In Germany, for example, it is not unknown for Eiswein grapes to be harvested in the early days of January.

Vintage Chart A 'scoreboard' showing the rating of wines from various countries and regions in different vintages. They are featured in some retailers' lists, and provide a reasonable guide for the consumer, though they are necessarily very generalized.

Vintage port The wine of one exceptionally fine vintage. Unlike other port styles, it is the wine of a single year, although it may be made from wines produced on a number of different estates. The decision as to whether a vintage should be 'declared' is in the hands of the shipper, and it is not unknown for only a handful of shippers to 'declare' in any one year, while in other years the majority will do so. Most Vintage ports are marketed under the shipper's name, though in recent years there has been a tendency for shippers to 'declare' a vintage for his best estate (or *quinta*) only, and market the wine under the name of the estate. Quinta do Noval is an example. Vintage port is bottled after two or three years in cask, and thereafter it requires anything from 10 to 30 years in bottle to become mellow.

Late-bottled Vintage port is a wine of one good year, or a blend of several good years, but spends between three and six years in cask, which has the effect of accelerating its development. Generally, Late-bottled Vintage port and 'vintage character' are ready to drink as soon as they have been bought.

vintage wine The wine of a single year. The term is sometimes misconstrued as being synonymous with fine and, implicitly, expensive wine.

Every year, however, is a vintage year, in the sense that harvesting or vintaging takes place each year, and even in the best regions it will only be fine if the year has been a particularly good one. In Champagne and in the port-wine region of Portugal the situation is different; here producers 'declare' a vintage only if the wine, after it has been made, shows special promise of greatness. The wines of other years are blended to make, in the case of Champagne, non-vintage, (NV) wine, and in the case of port to make Ruby or other plain styles. This approach has been adopted by a number of producers of light wines in France.

In general, the chances of buying a wine from a poor vintage in the UK are slender, since wine shippers do not buy them.

Viognier A white grape variety, a speciality of the Rhône Valley where it produces some of the region's finest wines.

Viré *(France)* Good, dry, fresh white wines from Mâcon, among the best of the area's whites.

Volnay *(France)* A very good wine commune of the Côte de Beaune. Most of its wine is red, of a generally high average quality, soft, flowery and smooth-textured. Les Caillerets and Champans are among the best properties. Some white wine is also made; it is entitled to the appellation Meursault.

Vosne-Romanée *(France)* A very fine red wine commune of the Côte de Nuits, with a reputation for producing wines of great elegance, powerful bouquet and rich flavour. Even the lesser wines of the commune, sold simply as Vosne-Romanée, have a share of these characteristics. The renowned vineyards are La Romanée, Romanée-Conti, Richebourg, La Tâche and La Romanée St-Vivant.

Vougeot *(France)* Admirable red wine commune of the Côte de Nuits. It also produces a limited quantity of good dry white, Clos Blanc de Vougeot. Its most famous property is the Clos de Vougeot, the largest of all Burgundian vineyards, whose best wine in a good year is round, soft and very stylish. The property, however, is owned in parcels by some 70 different proprietors, each responsible for the care of his own plot, so that even in a good year the wines of Clos de Vougeot can be variable.

Vouvray *(France)* A versatile white wine made in the district of Vouvray in the Loire region from the Chenin grape. In a vintage following a warm summer Vouvray can be very sweet but in other years, depending on the weather, it may be very dry or semi-sweet. The style most often encountered in Britain is medium dry. It is always a fresh, fruity wine and sometimes it can be *pétillant*. Much Vouvray is made into sparkling wine by the champagne method, and is one of the most outstanding sparkling wines of France.

Wachau *(Austria)* District near Vienna making fresh, flowery white wines. The most notable vineyards are round the town of Krems on the Danube, where the important Austrian Grüner Veltliner grape performs well.

Wachenheim *(Germany)* Notable wine district of the Rheinpfalz region. Wachenheim wines are nearly always light, with considerable finesse. The best districts in the locality include Gerümpel, Rechbächel, Luginsland and Altenberg.

Wehlen *(Germany)* The unassuming possessor of some of the finest wine sites in the Mosel regions, with distinguished white wines made from the Riesling grape.

White port Made only from white grapes, White port is light in colour but not in flavour. Some is sweet, but there are dry versions on the market, though they are never wholly dry.

Wiltingen (*Germany*) An outstanding wine commune of the Saar region, with a reputation for producing, in a good year, wines that are of a higher standard than those of many of the better Mosel vineyards. The finest vineyard is Scharzhofberg; others of distinction include Braune Kupp, Kupp and Gottesfuss.

wine aperitifs Herbs and other flavours are used to make these drinks, which are usually, but not always, sweet. Many contain quinine, to impart a balancing degree of bitterness. They are raised to an alcoholic strength some way above the standard strength of light wines. Among brand names are Dubonnet, St-Raphaël, and Byrrh. Most are available in red and white versions, the whites usually being lighter in flavour.

wine cup A cooling drink, made from red, white or rosé wine, usually with the addition of soda. lemonade or other soft drinks, and normally embellished with fruit, especially oranges and lemons, and sometimes cucumber.

Winkel (*Germany*) A little town in the Rheingau

region. Its principal and most famous vineyard is Schloss Vollrads, a property which produces exquisite wines of the best Rheingau character.

Worms *(Germany)* A small city in the Rheinhessen region. Its claim to fame is that the vineyards of Liebfrauenstift surround one of the city's churches and these were the vineyards that gave their name to Liebfraumilch which today, under German wine law, can come from much further afield. The Liebfrauenstift vineyards continue to produce wine, but it is not regarded as anything more than an average wine in the region.

Würzburg *(Germany)* The most important town and wine district of Franconia, producing aromatic, sometimes spicy wines of good quality. Würzburg is the home of the Stein vineyard, which gave its name to Steinwein, still erroneously applied to all the wines of Franconia. This is the most famous vineyard, but the Leiste vineyards produce wines of a comparable quality. Other notable names include Pfaffenberg and Schlossberg.

Yugoslavia A country which is a significant producer of a variety of wine styles, the best known of which in the UK market is Riesling.

This is a medium-dry white wine of sound quality made from the Italian Riesling grape. Other white grape varieties include Sylvaner, which makes good, medium-bodied dry wine, Traminer, a fruity, well-rounded wine which is usually medium-dry, and Sauvignon, firm, dry and fruity. Late-gathered grapes from the Ranina estate in the district of Lutomer are used to make the sweet wine marketed under the name Tiger Milk.

Red wines from Yugoslavia do not have as extensive a following in the UK as do whites, but interest among British shippers is growing and reds available include Cabernet Sauvignon, full-bodied and hearty.

Zeltingen *(Germany)* Village of the Mosel region, situated in the renowned Mittel-Mosel area, and centre of one of the best-rated wine districts in the region. Styles range from light, delicate wines to some of the fullest bodied of all Moselles. Important vineyard names include Sonnenuhr, Himmelreich and Schlossberg.

Zinfandel *(USA)* Californian red wine, named after the grape variety from which it is pressed. The name does not occur elsewhere in the wine-growing world, and although the vine is not native to America, its precise origins are unknown. It is believed to be a transplant from Europe. The wines it produces are generally undistinguished.

Zwicker *(France)* A blend of white wines produced in Alsace. Dry, fresh, usually with a good showing of fruit, the main wine in the blend is pressed from the productive Chasselas grape and the other, in small quantities, is pressed from the Sylvaner. Often sold under a brand name, it makes an agreeable quaffing wine at a fairly modest price. See also **Edelzwicker**.

Vintage Chart to Show Maturity

This table gives only an average indication of the wines of each vintage. The rate at which wine matures depends upon its quality, balance and type. The average quality of each vintage is marked out of a total of seven.

	1949	1950	1952	1953	1955	1957	1958	1959	1960
Port	—	5/DW	—	—	6/DW	—	5/DW	—	6/DW
Claret	6/SA	5/SA	6/DW	6/DW	5/DW	5/DW	4/SA	6/DW	5/DW
Burgundy	7/SA	4/SA	6/SA	6/SA	5/SA	5/SA	3/SA	6/SA	4/SA
Rhône	6/SA	6/SA	6/SA	6/SA	7/SA	6/SA	5/SA	6/SA	5/SA
Rhine and Moselle	7/SA	—	6/SA	7/SA	5/SA	5/SA	—	7/SA	—
Sauternes	5/SA	4/SA	6/SA	7/SA	7/SA	5/SA	—	7/SA	4/SA
White Burgundy	6/SA	—	6/SA	6/SA	6/SA	5/SA	—	7/SA	4/SA
Loire	6/SA	—	5/SA	6/SA	6/SA	5/SA	—	7/SA	5/SA
Champagne	—	—	—	7/SA	6/SA	—	—	7/SA	—

NR = Not Ready   RS = Ready Soon   JR = Just Ready
RN = Ready Now   DW = Drinking Well   SA = Showing Age
Red wines in particular are at their most attractive when they begin to
show age in bottle.
While Beaujolais vintages are usually comparable with those of Burgundy, the wines develop more quickly and can be drunk within a year of
the vintage.

1961	1962	1963	1964	1966	1967	1968	1969	1970	
—	5/RN	7/RS	—	7/NR	7/NR	—	—	7/NR	Port
7/JR	5/DW	3/SA	6/DW	6/DW	5/DW	3/DW	4/DW	6/JR	Claret
6/SA	5/DW	—	5/SA	6/DW	5/DW	3/SA	6/DW	6/DW	Burgundy
6/DW	6/DW	4/SA	6/SA	6/DW	6/DW	4/SA	6/DW	6/DW	Rhône
5/SA	4/SA	—	5/SA	5/SA	4/SA	—	6/SA	6/SA	Rhine and Moselle
6/SA	5/DW	—	4/SA	5/SA	6/DW	—	5/DW	6/DW	Sauternes
6/SA	5/SA	—	5/SA	6/SA	5/SA	—	5/SA	6/DW	White Burgundy
6/SA	5/SA	—	7/SA	6/SA	5/SA	—	6/SA	6/SA	Loire
7/SA	—	—	7/SA	7/DW	—	—	5/DW	6/RN	Champagne

We would like to thank John Harvey and Sons Limited of Bristol for their permission to reproduce this chart.

	1971	1972	1973	1974	1975	1976	1977	1978
Port	—	—	—	—	7/NR	—	6-NR	—
Claret	7/JR	3/DW	5/DW	4/DW	6/NR	6/JR	3/RS	6/NR
Burgundy	6/DW	5/DW	5/DW	5/DW	4/DW	7/NR	3/RS	7/NR
Rhône	6/DW	6/DW	5/DW	5/RN	4/RN	6/RS	4/NR	7/NR
Rhine and Moselle	7/DW	4/SA	5/DW	4/SA	5/DW	7/DW	4/DW	4/RS
Sauternes	6/DW	3/DW	3/DW	—	6/JR	6/RS	—	6/NR
White Burgundy	6/DW	5/DW	6/DW	6/DW	4/DW	6/RN	4/RN	6/NR
Loire	7/DW	6/DW	6/DW	6/DW	6/DW	6/DW	4/RN	6/RS
Champagne	5/RN	—	6/JR	—	7/NR	—	—	—